Who Is Jesus?

WHO IS JESUS?

by

GEORGE W. TRUETT, D.D., LL.D.

Compiled and Edited by
Powhatan W. James, Th.D., D.D.

BAKER BOOK HOUSE
Grand Rapids, Michigan

PHOTOLITHOPRINTED BY CUSHING - MALLOY, INC.
ANN ARBOR, MICHIGAN, UNITED STATES OF AMERICA
1 9 7 3

DEDICATION

This and other volumes
of sermons and addresses
in this series by Dr. George W. Truett
are dedicated to
his beloved
First Baptist Church, Dallas, Texas,
where most of them
were delivered

FOREWORD

This volume, Number VI in *The Truett Memorial Series,* is composed of fourteen sermons of the late Dr. George W. Truett, for forty-seven years pastor of the First Baptist Church, Dallas, Texas. These sermons all deal with the Person, the Mission and the Message of Jesus Christ — themes that were ever central in the ministry of this gospel preacher. The question asked in the title of the first sermon of this volume finds answer and abundant illustration in the fourteen sermons herein.

George W. Truett will long be remembered for a number of things that characterized the man and his ministry. Supreme among these things was his firm faith that Jesus Christ is the Son of God, the Saviour of the world, and the one rightful Lord and Master of men. This faith gave color and character to every sermon he ever preached. That explains why the multitudes heard him gladly. Faith is the victory that overcomes the world, for people hunger for the certitudes of faith.

It may be that many will be helped by looking at Jesus through the eyes of His devoted friend and follower, George W. Truett.

                                        Powhatan W. James

Dallas, Texas,
May 1, 1952

TABLE OF CONTENTS

CHAPTER I

Who Is Jesus?

Who Is Jesus?

~~~~~~

Truly this was the Son of God.
—MATTHEW 27:54.

I SPEAK to you from this statement in Matthew, the utterance of the centurion as he witnessed the death of Christ upon the cross: "Truly this was the Son of God." There have been only three views in the world as to Jesus of Nazareth. One view has been that He was a bad man. Another, that He was a good man, but utterly mad. And still another that He was what He claimed to be — the Son of God. These three views are the only ones that can be held. There cannot be any other. They comprehend all the notions of men, from the day of Christ's birth until this present hour.

Three views: One that He was bad, a blasphemer, not to be believed, nor trusted, nor honored at all. Caiphas, the high priest, before whom Jesus was arraigned, declared Him to be a blasphemer, worthy of death. That is one view. Another view was, and is, that He was a good man, but utterly mad, thoroughly deceived, utterly unbalanced. Pilate held to the view that He was good. "I find no fault in him," was the testimony of Governor Pilate, when Jesus was arraigned before him. And then, the centurion uttered the statement of our text, when he beheld the crucifixion. When he saw the marvelous manifestations of nature suffering and sympathizing in that dread hour, he cried out at last: "Truly this was the Son of God." There have been only three views, and these comprehend all from time to eternity. Let us examine them.

Was Jesus mad? Will it be seriously claimed now, that Jesus was mad? The wisest men of earth will not make that claim. The most pronounced unbelievers of earth will not make that claim. With uncovered head any man of sense, any man whose opinion on anything is worth listening to — with uncovered head, he will say: "Jesus was the fairest of all earth's men, and his teachings the sublimest, the most glorious." Any man who would not say that is not worth listening to on any subject and I dare say you would not stop to listen to him.

With uncovered head, the great men of the earth, whether saint or sinner, whether believer or doubter, have said that the teachings of Jesus Christ stamp Him as earth's wisest man; as earth's most perfect man, as earth's most prudent man. The Sermon on the Mount stands out even today as the most arresting discourse that ever fell on human ears. I am not surprised that Daniel Webster said: "A man, simply a man, only a man, could not be the author of such a sermon."

The "golden rule" uttered by Jesus stamps Him as the wisest person the world has seen. Just the golden rule. "Do unto others, as you would have others do unto you" is a statement that the world never approximated, in any shape, fashion or form, until it was enunciated by Jesus Christ. Men will hardly claim now, with seriousness, that Jesus was a hair-brained madman, as some of them did claim in other generations.

Was Jesus bad? Was the statement of the high priest justifiable, that Jesus was a blasphemer; that He was bad, and not to be trusted at all? Very few from that self-same day have made the assertion that Jesus was bad. Very few. I know of no man in all the world today who has the audacity to make the claim that Jesus of Nazareth was bad. Strange indeed is the man who would take up the things that Jesus uttered and make the declaration that these were emanations from a bad mind, a bad heart, a bad life. Even His foes are now uniform in their testimony that Jesus was good.

Just a little before he died, Mr. Ingersoll, who seemed to be the least likely man of the race to say anything good about Jesus, said: "After all, he was indeed good; and his was a life crowned with the teachings of his life, and the practice of his teaching harmonizing." Ingersoll was one of the last men in the world to be expected to offer a testimony as to the good character of the Lord Jesus. All of Jesus' foes are agreed now in their testimony that He stands out among earth's men, higher than the highest, unrivaled, unmatched, unapproached by any other born of woman. There is little conflict of testimony or opinion on that point, today.

If Jesus Christ was not mad, and if He was not bad, then He was what He claimed to be. He was God incarnate. It will not do for a man to say that He was good, but not God. The Jew or any other man who compliments Jesus and stops at that gets himself into interminable difficulties. Jesus was bad or He was good. Jesus was good, and if He was good, He was God; for when you examine the claims that Jesus made respecting Himself, if those claims were not true, literally, unqualifiedly, absolutely, then Jesus was the arch imposter of all the ages. He was not only a deceiver, but He was earth's arch deceiver of the children of men; an arch deceiver, a willful deceiver as to the things most meaningful that can ever be considered by the minds and hearts of men. No sane man can call in question that Jesus was utterly good. And, if utterly good, then Jesus was God; for His claims all go to naught and He stands out, I repeat, as a blasphemer, as earth's arch deceiver, if He was not literally what He claimed to be.

Now, look for a moment at the claims of Jesus. He declared that He came down from Heaven on a mission for a little while here on the earth; that He came on that mission to do the will of His heavenly Father, to seek and to save the lost by making atonement for the sins of all who would believe on Him and follow Him. He declared that He was the way, and the truth, and the life; and that no one could come unto

15

the Father except by Him. That was His uniform testimony and declaration.

Jesus often referred to Himself as the Son of man. Not *a* son of man, but *the* son of man. Not a son of a Jew, nor the son of a Greek, nor the son of a Roman, but of universal humanity. And, in His life, He illustrated that great claim. He rose above His environment. He grew up in a little town. He never went out of His own country, Palestine, after His babyhood, and yet, Jesus was the universal man. He did not resemble a Jew any more than He resembled a Greek; any more than He resembled a Roman; yet Jesus was a Jew. No race or nation can claim Him exclusively. He belongs to all. Jesus is earth's universal man. He was in frequent conflict with the Jewish people on account of their racial prejudices, their religious bigotry and their social exclusiveness. They despised the Greeks and Romans and all other peoples, and were despised in return.

He declared: "I am the son of man," and then He went on to declare more than that — "I am the son of God." I have been surprised to read various statements from doubters, who rise up and insist that Jesus never had the audacity to declare that He was the son of God. They only advertise their utter ignorance of the Word of God. Repeatedly Jesus declared: "I am the son of God, the Almighty." He said it to the high priest when arraigned before him for trial. The high priest put Him on oath: "I adjure thee, by the living God, tell me whether thou be the Christ, the Son of God, as you claim to be," and He answered: "Thou hast said." And then the high priest rent his clothes and declared that He must be put to death; that He was a blasphemer, and for that blasphemy He must be put to death. Jesus with His eyes wide open, knowing the Jewish law, said that He was the son of God. He declared that self-same thing to the high priest. And when Pilate, the governor, wanted to release Him, the crowd clamored back the cry: "Nay we cannot release him, because he has affirmed that he is the son of God, and he must be put to death."

When He was on the cross, His enemies stood and taunted Him: "Let him save himself now, if he can. He claims that he is the son of God. Surely the son of God can save himself. Let him now show the people his infinite power." And all of the inspired writers bore testimony that Jesus was the Son of God. The apostle John bore that testimony again and again. "John saw and bear record that Jesus was the son of God." It was the burden of that apostle's message everywhere: "He is Jesus, the Christ, the Son of God." And the centurion, witnessing that awful struggle, the death of Jesus on the cross, cried out at last and gave his testimony: "Surely he was the son of God."

Jesus not only claimed that He was the son of God, but He claimed identity with God the Father. Time and time again that was the declaration from His earnest, honest, candid lips, that He was God. Time and again, He said to the people: "You talk about God the Father. I say unto you, he that hath seen me hath seen the Father. I am in the Father and the Father in me: I and my Father are one. I was with him yonder before the worlds were."

Time and again, that was the assertion that came from His lips; and it shows that He claimed attributes which belong only to an Infinite God. For Himself He claimed the attribute of eternity. One day, when they quibbled and talked to Him about Abraham, long dead, hundreds and hundreds of years, He said: "You talk about Abraham. I ante-date Abraham. Long before Abraham was, I was. I preceded him." And then, again in one of His prayers, there came the expression: "Father glorify me now on earth, as I pray, with the glory which I had with thee before the worlds were."

Jesus was for a season down here in the flesh, and He not only claimed to be God's son, and God Himself manifest in the flesh, but He asserted that in Himself there were the attributes of Jehovah. He claimed omnipotent power. They brought around Him their sick, their diseased, their sinful,

17

and He said: "By a word I can heal your sick," and He did it. And He said, "By a word I can cleanse you from your sins," and He did it. And He said: "By a word I can raise your dead men," and He did it.

Jesus Christ, I repeat, was utterly bad or He was God. Would a bad man teach the lessons that He taught, and make the statements that He made? Jesus is one of the three things claimed. He was mad, or He was bad, or He was God. By His own divine claims, He made the assertion of His divinity. He asserted His omnipresence to His disciples, when He made the statement: "Where two or three are gathered together in my name, there am I in the midst of them." And again, "Lo, I will be with you always, even unto the end of the world."

Jesus claimed to be the antidote for all the evils and sorrows of men, the panacea for all the afflictions of the children of men. Wonderful audacity! Compare His claims with the claims of others. Others talk about rules, about systems, about creeds, about philosophy: Jesus stands out before men and declares: "I am God. Salvation is in me; not in a creed, not in a system, not in a philosophy, not in a church. Salvation is in me." And He stands out unmatched and unrivaled in that very assertion. "I am the bread of life. I am life for men. I am the way, the truth and the life. I am the door into heaven for men. I will give them rest and peace and cleansing and eternal salvation, if they will come to me."

Those were claims that Jesus everywhere made. Were they claims of a madman? Were they claims of a bad man? Such claims were utterly false unless they came from the lips of One to whom all authority in heaven and on earth hath been given. If Jesus Christ was only a man, then we have the spectacle of a man, nineteen hundred years ago going infinitely beyond the thought of the wisest men of that age, of any other age. And it is utterly inconceivable that the Jesus of the Scriptures was only a figment of the imagination of the men who wrote the inspired Word of God. Jesus Christ was and is an eternal reality — the God-man, the one perfect union of the divine and the human, the Son of God and the Son of man. In other words, Jesus of Nazareth was God incarnate in human form.

There can be no doubt that Jesus claimed divinity for Himself and His mission!

Now, let us consider the personality of Jesus Christ. There have been men who made adroit attempts to show that there was no such person as Jesus of Nazareth. A number of attempts have been made to show that Jesus was a myth, that He never lived at all. There is no need of argument with men of that class. They are blinded by prejudice and are not capable of weighing evidence or reaching a logical conclusion based on incontrovertible evidence.

No candid and capable mind will call in question that Jesus of Nazareth lived and journeyed, and ate, and talked, and preached, and died on the cross, just as the Bible affirms. No candid, capable man would even think of calling that in question. Unbelievers are sure to get themselves into interminable difficulties right there. Strauss and Tremaine and Spencer and Gilbert and others declare that the man was undoubtedly perfect, but they find themselves in the mazes as they deny His divinity; for they have a perfect man, asserting that He was God; asserting that He came down from heaven; asserting that He came to lift up a fallen world; asserting His eternal existence; claiming for Himself both omnipotence and omnipresence.

Those men who place a chaplet on the brow of Jesus and say that He was the wisest, the most prudent, and the best of all earth's men — if their theory be true, are putting their chaplet upon the most consummate blasphemer, imposter and falsifier that earth ever saw.

The personality of Jesus is a proof of His divinity. Otherwise the great civilizations of the world would not have reckoned time from the day of the coming of Jesus. Every business man today gives acknowledgment of the fact of Jesus' divinity in every letter that he sends out in the mail. Anno Domini, A. D., means "in the year of our Lord." Every civil-

19

ization on the earth reckons dates from the time that divinity left heaven for a few years to dwell among men, to show them the way back to God. All state papers in every land, all legal papers and every date of importance in the world of letters are reckoned from that same date.

I would have you look not only at Jesus' personality, but I would have you look also at His character. His character stands out before us by universal consent as absolutely flawless. I have searched earnestly in these latter years to find one man who had the audacity to criticize the character of Jesus Christ; and it stands out just as Pilate affirmed: "I find no fault in him." And you remember, Jesus, in effect, said to men, when He was on the earth: "I am free from sin."

A character without spot or blemish or wrinkle or flaw! Who owned that character? Compare Jesus with other men. O, friends, if Jesus was only a man, why cannot other men reach perfection? Look at Moses! whose great brain formulated the principles of law and government and education, which principles live on today, and yet, Moses sinned egregiously, time and again, and the record is put down in this Book of God. David was the man who greatly pleased God in his life — and yet, the time came when he coveted Uriah's lamb and brought shame unspeakable upon his name and upon his entire kingdom. Look at Elijah, that mighty champion of righteousness, who on Carmel's heights defeated and slew the hundreds of false prophets; the man who prayed and in answer thereto the fire came down from heaven; and yet, who in a panic of cowardice fled into a far country, because of the threat of a wicked woman.

Look at Paul, the apostle, and Barnabas, his friend. These two fell out and had a fierce quarrel and separated. But Jesus is One in whom no man can find mote, or spot, or defect, or blemish. And no man can justly bring one single accusation against the character of Jesus of Nazareth. That very fact is a demonstration overwhelming, that the perfect Man was what He claimed to be — God as well as man.

Look also, I pray you, at His teaching. "Never man spake like this man." He spoke with the voice of authority in His every utterance. The teachers of His day, and of every other day, must quote the sayings of others to establish the authority of their own teachings. Not so did Jesus speak. His words were always: "I say unto you." He stood out and talked about the great law of vengeance, which was in the old Mosaic law. The old law was "an eye for an eye, and a life for a life." "Not so my law," said Jesus. "Recompense not evil for evil, but instead, return good for evil." The teachings of Jesus were another proof of His divinity.

Look at His works. That was a great argument Christ made when the people would not believe Him. He said: "If you will not believe me, I pray you, believe me for my very work's sake." Was it not a telling argument? If you will not believe in me, then, look, see what I do, and believe in me. If some man comes to tell me that Jesus of Nazareth did not rise from the dead literally, as the Scriptures affirm, then I answer him: "Jesus Christ has as much power in the earth today, as if He did rise from the dead." Jesus Christ died over nineteen hundred years ago, and millions today would offer their lives a willing sacrifice on His altar. Napoleon talked like a man of sense to one of his marshals. He asked him: "Who was Jesus of Nazareth?" and the marshal answered back that he could not tell him, and Napoleon said: "If you do not know that Jesus of Nazareth was God, I made a mistake in making you one of my marshals." Later on, Napoleon said: "I build up great empires by the point of the sword. Jesus built an empire, not on swords, but upon love, and though He has been dead over eighteen hundred years, millions of men would fight for that man, so long dead." Said Napoleon: "If you cannot understand that He was more than man, I made a mistake in making you my marshal." Christ's works in the earth demonstrated His divinity.

Look at His mission. He came with a new mission. Jesus did not come to be a reformer. Jesus came to be a former. "Behold I make all things new," was the utterance of Jesus of Nazareth. Others built on many things. Mohammed built on false hope. Mormonism builds on its system of laws. All heathen religions build on false foundations. "I come to make all things new," was the voice of this new teacher in the earth. And here you have the spectacle of One, not following the teaching of any school or college, who wrote but one line while in the world, so far as we know, and that was written on the ground, in the presence of an unfortunate woman's accusers: and yet we have the spectacle of One whose teachings reshape the world.

Let us notice His own statement: "I will come to Jerusalem, and I will be slain there, and they will bury me, and in three days I will rise from the grave, and my death shall be the great sign of victory forever." Christ did not point men to His transfiguration mountain, when the old mountain was lighted up with glory; but He pointed them to His death as the transaction whereby the world should be saved. Christ took what men called defeat, utter defeat, overwhelming defeat; and, out of that, said: "I will win the world." Men do not build monuments to their defeats. The French have never erected a monument to the battle of Waterloo. But Jesus built a monument to what men call His defeat, and out of that monument, even His death, He proposes to take the world for Himself.

What of the success of His mission? As the light dispels darkness, Jesus has gone on conquering the darkness of earth. Julian the Emperor issued his edicts, but Christ went on. Hume, the philosopher, wrote his philosophies, but Christ went on. Voltaire, the unbeliever, sneered at Christ, but Christ went on. Ingersoll prated all over the land, but Christ went on, conquering and to conquer, in all climes and races and conditions of the sons of men.

The centurion was right. Jesus was the Son of God. Jesus was what He claimed to be. Jesus came from heaven to the earth for a brief season, to reconcile a lost world to God. Do you doubt it? Will you tell me He was a poor, deluded man? O, do you doubt the divine claims of Jesus? The supreme question for human thought in every age is this: What do you think of Jesus Christ? And with that I close, adding simply this other question: If Jesus is God, what are you going to do with Him? What are you going to do with Him? Accept Him, friend, as your Saviour and the Redeemer of your lost soul! Accept Him now and confess Him in the presence of this host of His friends. That will bring joy to the Saviour's heart and to your own heart and to the hearts of these His friends; and the angels in heaven will be made to rejoice. Yes, I believe that it will also add to the joys of your redeemed loved ones who have gone on before. God help you to accept and confess Christ now, as we sing: "All hail the power of Jesus' name."

CHAPTER II

The Mission of Jesus

CHAPTER I I

The Mission of Jesus

~~~~~~

> *And all bare him witness, and won-
> dered at the words of grace which
> proceeded out of his mouth.*
>
> —LUKE 4:22.

AN ACCOUNT of the first sermon Jesus preached
in His home synagogue is found in the fourth chapter of
Luke's Gospel. Jesus had come back to Nazareth and on the
Sabbath day He went into the synagogue to worship as was
His custom. From early childhood He had been going to the
synagogue when the Sabbath day came, there to worship.

Jesus had already made a tour in His public ministry away
from His own community, and news of that tour had doubtless
provoked a great deal of wonder and curious inquiry upon the
part of the people among whom He had been reared. And
now the day had arrived when Jesus had returned from that
tour in other places and had come again to His own village,
and again to the synagogue where, with His companions
through the years, He had worshipped.

On this Sabbath day the leader of the synagogue handed
Jesus the book of the prophet Isaiah and He stood and read
a famous passage found in the sixty-first chapter of Isaiah.
Then He closed the book and sat down, as was the custom of
teachers. They stood when they read from the law; they sat
down when they taught. When Jesus had thus closed the
book and seated Himself, He looked upon that throng and
said, "This day is this scripture fulfilled in your ears."

What surprise must have been on their faces when they
heard that statement! Remember that this was His first ser-

mon to His home-town people. That is an important event for any preacher! You can picture Mary there with glowing eyes and fast-beating heart as she listened to Him. In fancy you can see the men and women with whom He had played as a child. No doubt the synagogue was crowded that day. Some heard Him, I doubt not, with profoundest sympathy, others with mere curiosity, and others, perhaps, with jealousy, and still others may have heard Him contemptuously in that village synagogue that day.

Every young preacher remembers his first sermon to his own home folk. He remembers everything about it — the songs the people sang, and how they looked up into his face as he stammered and got through, he scarcely knew how, that first effort. If it will be pardonable to make such reference I will say that when I came to preach my first sermon it was only thirteen minutes long. I preached on that great text from Jesus: "Ye are the light of the world." In thirteen minutes I said all I knew to say on that text. But I shall never forget the faces of the people and their warm hand-clasps when it was over and how one after another said, "I prayed for you. I love you. I helped you all I could." That first sermon to the home folk is a great occasion in the life of any preacher.

The passage which Jesus read and which He said was being fulfilled that day was this: "The Spirit of the Lord is upon me, because he hath anointed me to preach the gospel to the poor; he hath sent me to heal the broken-hearted, to preach deliverance to the captives, and recovering of sight to the blind, to set at liberty them that are bruised." And when Jesus had finished, while the eyes of all the congregation were fixed upon Him, He said, "This day is this Scripture fulfilled in your ears."

The Scripture states clearly the mission of Jesus to mankind. As a prelude He began by stating the first great requisite for the true preacher of God: "The Spirit of the

Lord is upon me because he hath anointed me to preach." Oh, that is the prime and indispensable requisite for the preacher. It is important for the preacher to be an informed man, to be a trained man. But, oh, of prime importance, the supreme requisite for the preacher of the glorious gospel of Christ is that he shall be a man anointed by the Divine Spirit for His work, for His messages, for His ministry.

Without ceasing men and women who desire that the kingdom of Christ shall triumph in the earth need to pray that the same Spirit Divine who rested upon Jesus when He preached in the synagogue at Nazareth may rest upon all preachers who preach Christ's gospel. The true preacher's task is a divine vocation. He is sent of God. He is called of God. He is anointed of God for His work. Pray then, all you who desire the triumph of God's kingdom which is the world's hope, that Spirit-called men may come, as God wills, to preach the gospel with the power of God sent down from above. Jesus began His sermon by saying, "The Spirit of the Lord is upon me, because he hath anointed me to preach."

There are several thoughts in this passage which emphasize Jesus' mission. First: "He hath anointed me to preach the gospel to the poor." That deserves to come first, "to preach the gospel to the poor." Oh, a new thing was sounded in the earth when Jesus said, "I came to preach the gospel." What does the word "gospel" mean? It means "good news." Isaiah characterized it as "glad tidings." "I came," said Jesus, "to preach good news. I came to proclaim glad tidings." And what is the good news Jesus came to preach? Jesus came to preach the gospel of salvation, of salvation by grace, of salvation as a gift. Before Jesus came the world was filled with the doctrine of doing, the doctrine of salvation by merit, of salvation by works of righteousness, which men could do. Then Jesus came saying, "I come with good news. I come with glad tidings. I come with a pardon for every sinner who will consent for me to be his Saviour. I come

29

with the gift of eternal life for every sinner on the earth, who will accept it from my hands, yielding life and all to my guidance and government."

That was a new note in the world. The last note of every pagan religion is self-reliance. The first note of the Christian religion is reliance on God. Jesus came with divine help, with divine succor, with divine reinforcement, with divine mercy, with divine salvation, to a world broken and beaten and tossed and shattered. In such an hour Jesus came, saying, "My task is to preach the gospel to the poor."

One glory of the gospel of Jesus Christ is that it is adapted to the needs of all men everywhere. The rise of the plain people has come wherever the gospel of Jesus had been faithfully proclaimed. The glory of His gospel is that the common people heard Him gladly when He was here in the flesh; and the common people hear Him gladly now. After all, the common people are the hope of this world, because there are so many of them. Jesus came with a gospel for the poor, a divine gospel for the poor in purse and for the poor in spirit.

On the other hand, many of the teachings of Jesus Christ were specially adapted to the moral and spiritual needs of the rich, prominent and powerful. What Jesus said to the rich young ruler who came asking what he should do in order that he might inherit eternal life is a case in point. Jesus loved this young man and really coveted him for the kingdom of God. But when Jesus told him what, in his case, would be needful for him to do, he went away filled with sorrow because he valued his wealth and what it could do for him more than he valued the eternal life about which he had asked Jesus. The tragic choice of this rich young man prompted Jesus to point out the exceeding peril of riches and their power to enthrall men and bar the way into the kingdom of God. It was then that Jesus said to His disciples: "How hardly shall they that have riches enter into the kingdom of God! For it is easier for a camel to go through a needle's eye than for a rich man to enter into the kingdom of God . . . . With men it is impossible, but not with God: for all things are possible with God."

The parables of The Unjust Steward, The Rich Fool, Dives and Lazarus, The Pounds, all have lessons of vital interest for wealthy, highly placed business and professional people. It cannot be said too often that the gospel of Jesus Christ is for all classes and conditions of people.

The second phase of Christ's mission was stated thus: "He hath sent me to heal the broken-hearted." Oh, what a mission is that, "to heal the broken-hearted," for the broken-hearted are on every hand. Everywhere the sad undertone of the broken-hearted may be heard and the cry of their grief, of their heavy burdens, of their disappointments, comes to our ears continually. How many hearts are broken because they have failed, simply failed in life! And many people, measured by human standards, do fail.

Then there are the broken-hearted because of disappointments. Oh, the disappointed people that are in the world, the people beaten into the dust by the flail of unexpected and harassing disappointment, the people bereaved and broken-hearted because their plans have all failed. They are all about us, people who have come short of their goal, and they go with faces pallid from the very memory of certain experiences through which they have been called to pass, burdensome and shattering and terrible experiences. And then add to all this the deepest grief perhaps of all, the grief that comes when the home is shattered, as out of that home one is taken, and another, and another.

No matter what the cause, Jesus is able to heal each broken heart. He tells us in His Word: "I am the Lord that healeth them." Again we read: "He healeth the broken in heart." "Many are the afflictions of the righteous: but the Lord delivereth him out of them all." Whatever your sorrow, or deep, consuming grief, whatever your burden, whatever the pressure upon you, Jesus says, "Come unto me, all ye that labor and are heavy laden, and I will give you rest."

The third phase of Christ's mission was "to preach deliverance to the captives and to set at liberty them that are bruised." Jesus came to give liberty, to give freedom. Sin is slavery. Whoever follows sin is the servant of sin, and the worst master that man ever followed is Satan, the father of evil. Whoever follows sin is the slave of sin, the servant of sin, the bond-servant of sin. Jesus said, "I came to break those shackles. I came to recover the servant of sin and Satan from his yoke, from his bondage, from his fearful serfdom. I came to set him free. I came to put him in my kingdom. I came to take him out of the kingdom of darkness and put him in the kingdom of light. I came to save him from sin to righteousness, to save him from selfishness to usefulness, to save him from waste to service, to save him from the wrong to the right, to save him from hell to heaven, to save him here and now. I came to give him the abundant life. I came to set him free, that he should not be the servant of the cruelest master that ever put his chains about a human neck or a human heart, Satan, the despoiler of mankind. I came to set him free."

The tragedy of the world is sin. The one obtruding fact in the world today is the fact of sin. The one galling yoke on human necks and hearts in the world today is the yoke of sin. Jesus came to remove that yoke. Jesus came to break those shackles. Jesus came to set men free, and to put their feet on the solid Rock, Himself, the Divine Saviour. Whoever comes to Him receives deliverance, forgiveness, redemption, salvation.

There is a fourth phase of Jesus' mission. He came to give recovering of sight to them that are blind. He came to give vision. Sin is blindness. The Bible everywhere represents it as such. Sin is the most stupid thing in the wide world. There never was a sin that paid, from the first one in Eden to the last one committed in this hour. Sin is a cheat. Sin is a delusion. Sin is a pretender. Sin is ever a deceiver. Sin blinds. Sin utterly destroys vision. All sin carries with it a penalty, a burden, a retribution. Jesus came to give sight, to cause us to see. When we come to Him, and yield to Him, and surrender to Him, then it is He gives us to see, and we can say with that blind man whom Jesus healed: "Whereas I was blind, now I see." We can say with Paul, who called himself the chief of sinners: "I know whom I have believed, and am persuaded that he is able to keep that which I have committed unto him against that day."

Jesus came to give vision. How much there is in vision! How much there is in sight! The difference in people may be just there. Two people may look upon the same thing, and one sees practically nothing in it, and the other's heart burns and glows with what he sees. Mrs. Browning had a way of saying that every common bush about her was all aflame with God. Some men see and some do not. Jesus came to give men vision, to give men sight to follow the right way and forsake the wrong, to see the deadly peril that menaces, the retribution that always follows sin, and to see the victory and the triumph that always crown the upward way.

When Jesus said that day in the synagogue of Nazareth that He was the fulfillment of Isaiah's prophecy concerning the four-fold mission of Jehovah's anointed and suffering servant, He made a claim that was thoroughly vindicated by His subsequent mission and message. The gospel which Jesus proclaimed and practiced proved to be the perfect fulfillment of the Messiah, the Redeemer, the Suffering Servant, the Saviour, of Prophecy. Verily He did preach the gospel to the poor, He did heal the broken-hearted, He did proclaim liberty to the captives, He did give vision to the eyes of the blind. Yes, He did these things and much more when He was here in the flesh, and He has continued to do them from that day to this. If you will come to Him, trust Him, confess Him, He will open your eyes to see the awfulness of sin and the reality of salvation; He will heal your wounded and broken heart; He will give to you pardon, peace and power, yes, He will give you the assurance of eternal life.

Surely that is a gospel and Saviour worth accepting, worth preaching, worth living for, worth dying for. Have you accepted that Saviour to be yours? Have you let Him do for you what He wishes to do for you? Have you made surrender of yourself to Him, that He may forgive, and that He may deliver, and that He may change, and that He may give you the new heart and the new motive, and the new life, and the new impulse, and the new love, and the new power? Have you made surrender of yourself to Christ to be your personal Saviour? Make it now. Make it this very hour. Make it while we pray.

CHAPTER III

Jesus Our Confidant

CHAPTER III

Jesus Our Confidant

〜〜〜〜〜〜〜〜〜〜〜〜〜〜〜〜〜〜〜〜〜〜〜〜〜〜〜

> *And his disciples came, and took up the body, and buried it, and went and told Jesus.*
>
> —MATTHEW 14:12.

IT WAS the disciples of John the Baptist who went and told Jesus about the murder of their Master.

You will give yourselves, I trust, for a little while to a fresh and very earnest study of the character of this man, John the Baptist. Jesus said of him: "Among them that are born of women there hath not risen a greater than John the Baptist." Gaunt, stern, austere, and rigidly righteous, yet he was a man who was the center of a group of friends who were ready to die for him. He had convictions and stood by them without compromise and without betraying them under any pressure.

What a man was this herald of Jesus! This forerunner of the Saviour, John the Baptist. Let our young men devote themselves to the study of the right kind of men. Let them see character incarnated in worthy men. Let them see integrity resting upon worthy men gracefully, as some beautifully fitted garment.

John the Baptist was a man of such worthiness and such strength that the several paragraphs in the New Testament about him should call forth the keenest study and the most careful analysis from every man and woman among us. John the Baptist was so strong that, though he was stern and austere and rigidly righteous, though his meat was locusts and wild honey, though he was unique and peculiar, yet there was about him such massive strength that, like Peter the Hermit, or like Savonarola, or like Oliver Cromwell, he had a great following in his day. Why do men follow other men? How can men rally other men by the sheer impact of personal influence? Study John the Baptist and see these truths unfolded vividly.

Jesus appeared on the scene, after John had foretold His coming. When Jesus came the crowds fell away from John. John, for a season, had emptied the towns of their inhabitants. John, this rugged man from the hill country of Judea, spoke his wonderful words to the people out there by the riverside. Away from the crowded cities they followed him from near and far, to listen to the living, breathing, burning words that John was minded to speak.

But now Jesus has come and the tide turns, and those great crowds no longer follow John, but Jesus has them now. Then John's disciples, John's champions, John's comrades, John's enthusiasts, are filled with pain, because the tide has turned, and they say to John, their great leader: "This ought not to be. You have done your work faithfully and well. You have been the herald, the forerunner. Now Jesus seems to have your audience, seems to have your congregation, seems to have your followers, seems to have your fame." Then the great forerunner, John the Baptist, uttered the sentence that will live forever: "He must increase but I must decrease." Oh, what a sentence! What a tribute! What self-abnegation! What glorification of Christ!

Following that incident John was thrust into prison and his prison experience was followed by his tragic death. You remember, do you not, the setting for it all? John stood before Herod Antipas and said, in words pungent and biting: "It is not lawful, sir, for thee to have thy brother Philip's wife. Your relations to her are improper and incorrect, and those relations should cease. A man must make answer to God for the deeds done in the body, and you are piling up wrath against the day of wrath, as you go on in these evil and improper relations."

Herod winced under this, and the woman, Herodias, winced far more. She nursed her anger like some adder to her heart, and she bided her time. No man with his avenging eyes could look down into her face, and into the face of the man beside her, and say those words which burned like fire: "It is not lawful for thee to have her." No man could rebuke them without being summoned to the wreaking of her vengeance, if her opportunity ever came; and it came on apace.

Herod's birthday soon was celebrated, and he was feasted and flattered and congratulated. Wine flowed freely, and the senses were excited by the intoxicating cup. The daughter of Herodias, the girl Salome, came in and danced before Herod and his guests, and their physical senses were so stirred that they lost their judgment about it all, and Herod said to the girl: "Ask what you will, and I will give it to you. You have pleased me. You have delighted me. You have delighted these guests. Make any request that you would have of me, and you shall have it."

Salome had been prompted by her mother. That woman, biding her time; that same woman nursing her adder of anger and vengeance against John, said to her young daughter: "Tell Herod that nothing will suffice you except the head of John the Baptist, brought in a charger and put right before us." Now, think of a woman making that request!

We are having chapters now in human history that are as base and despicable and horrible as that, if we are to believe some of the reports which reach us from the great world conflict over the seas. But here was a woman, in time of peace, nearly two thousand years ago, who rivaled in cold-blooded cruelty the deeds done today in time of war!

The record here tells us that Herod was exceedingly sorry that he had made any such promise, but nevertheless, for his oath's sake and for the sake of those who sat at meat with him, he carried out that dreadful promise, "And his head was brought in a charger, and given to the damsel, and she brought it to her mother." When a man makes a bad mistake, he should retract it as soon as he discovers his mistake.

A group of men waited upon me a little while ago and said: "We have agreed to stand together about a certain matter." I said: "A deeper question than that is: Ought you to have made that agreement?" "Not at all"; they said. Then I said: "You ought to break it. It is not a debatable question. If you ought not to have made this agreement, then you ought to break it. You must not stand by a bad agreement, simply because back yonder a group covenanted together that, no matter what might come, you would stand by that original course of conduct."

If you have made a bad promise, if you have given an oath, if you have made a resolution that is unworthy and improper, break it, and say: "I break it because it is wrong. I break it because I know better now. I break it because I ought never to have made it at all, and now, having made it, and seeing it is wrong and improper, I break it."

Herod would not break his oath. He let it stand and sent an executioner to the dungeon where John was confined and had been for weeks. After a while the messenger came back with the head of John the Baptist, there in the charger as Salome requested. No more will those fiery eyes flash with indignation as he looks at Herod and Herodias. No more will that tongue, charged with condemnation, direct its fearful warning at the guilty couple. No more!

And yet, later, Herod was shot through with consternation and with fear by his conscience, for though the conscience was drugged, though the conscience was largely deadened, yet it came back and made its cry in the after days, even about that same John.

Now, that is the setting. When he was killed, John's disciples secured the body, and took it away and gave it a loving burial. Then, what could they do? There was but one place for them to go, and the text tells us: "They went and told Jesus."

That simple text suggests that occasions come to us in life, when the stress and the strain are on, when the battles and the burdens are heavy, occasions come in life when the only recourse for us, the only proper thing for us, is to go straightway to Jesus and talk it all over with Him. "They went and told Jesus."

Let us consider several occasions in life when you and I should make Him our confidant, and when we should bare our hearts before Him, when we should keep back nothing, when we should tell Him all and say: "Now that the case is stated, speak Thou Thy will; make plain Thy wish, and we will be found doing what Thou sayest."

Let us consider some of the occasions in which we should go to Jesus and tell Him what is in our hearts. First, we should go and tell Jesus when the day of sorrow comes, just as John's disciples went and told Jesus when their day of blinding, maddening, overpowering sorrow came. They went and told it all to Jesus. Even so, when you and I come to the day of sorrow, when the clouds come black robed, when the day of sorrow comes, the day of tears, the day of testing and tribulations, no matter how it is expressed, we shall make a sad mistake, if we refrain from going with it all to Jesus and saying: "Here is my sorrow. Here it is, Lord Jesus. Speak through it and reveal Thy will for us in it all." If we fail to do that, we shall indeed make a sad mistake.

My friends, in its last analysis, personal religion comes back to our relation to Christ. He comes calling us in cadences sweeter than ever came from a mother's lips: "Come unto me, all ye that labor and are heavy laden, and I will give you rest." He comes saying to us: "I, the Lord, change not. I am the same yesterday, today and forever. And therefore, I will be with you also even to the end. You are

41

to come to me, and to bring your trouble to me, and I will give light and leading. I will grant love and strength, and I will not forsake nor forget, in that hour of sorrow that comes."

Whatever the sorrow may be, we are to take that sorrow to Christ. Sorrow comes in different forms. It comes robed in many different garbs. Whatever the sorrow, we are to take that sorrow to Jesus and say: "Here, Lord, it is. Please manage it for us."

When Oliver Cromwell lay dying, it was a stormy night. The wind howled and shook the house until it seemed as if it would fall. After awhile great, old, rugged Cromwell said to the loved ones about him: "Read to me from Paul's letter to the Philippians. Read that to me." They read to him, and when they read that great verse: "I can do all things through Christ who strengtheneth me," he said: "Stop just there. That was the word that saved me. When my son, Oliver, died, that was the word that saved me. When my heart was broken, that was the word that saved me. When sorrow swept down on our home as a black vulture, that was the word that saved me. When in one short hour all my sun was hid in midnight darkness, that was the word that saved me — 'I can do all things through Christ who strengtheneth me.'"

And so, my friends, you can go to Christ and I can go, and ought to go, when trouble comes, no matter what form it assumes, no matter what guise or dress it wears, you can go to Him, and say: "Here am I Lord. Put thy hand on me. Put Thy Spirit in me. Make me to know that Thy promises are for me, and give me the sense of Thy grace, so that I shall be upborne, and shall not be afraid." And He will sustain you and give you the help you need.

Sometimes trouble comes because of a sad bereavement, occasioned by the going away of a loved one. It is so every week here, and never do I look down on this audience Sunday morning or night, but that I look into the faces of bereaved ones and read something of the chapters of tribulation and tears through which they have been called to pass, in recent days. As I look over this audience now there is one whose heart is terribly burdened because of the fearful sorrow that came in one short night.

And there is another, with an utterly different sorrow, coming from an utterly different angle. Bring it all to Christ. Bring it all to Christ and tell Him all. It may be sorrow occasioned by reverses in your business, by failure in your business plans, by the overturning of your programs. Bring all that to Christ.

Have you ever paused before a pawnbroker's shop and looked in the window for awhile? I have and I never did so except with a strange tug at my heart. The other day I paused there and noticed various and sundry things in that window for sale. You could "read between the lines." There was a little pair of shoes of some tiny baby; and there was a small shawl; and there was a violin, and on and on. In each case there was a suggestion of sacrifice and heartbreak. How full of human interest it all was! Bring your sorrow to Christ and say: "Here it is. Speak to me. Shine into my mind; it is so dark. Reinforce my heart; it is so fearful. Stir my will; it seems so weak." And He will come with deliverance and help.

Another occasion when we should go and tell Jesus is the very opposite of those I have just mentioned. We should go and tell Jesus in the day of success, all about our success, about the bright chapters, about the achievements, about the triumphs, about the things which stir our hearts with the sense of victory. We should tell Jesus about them, just as we tell Him in the dark and cloudy day when the battle seems lost.

If anybody preeminently needs to talk to Jesus, to get His counsel, it is the man who is prosperous. This truth should ever be sounded out clear and loud and long. The one who is prosperous needs to go and tell Jesus: "I need Thee. I

43

need Thy moderation. I need Thy modifying influence. I need Thy counsel. I need Thy light. I need Thy leading. I need Thee in all these chapters of prosperity which I am writing now in my little life."

Awhile ago, in one of our American cities, there was a young man who had come into the possession of much property, and a friend sent up to the minister on Sunday morning a note, saying: "Special prayers are asked for a young man who has come into the possession of much property. He is in great danger now. Let a special prayer be offered for him by the minister and the whole congregation." That request was altogether appropriate.

I once saw in another city, larger than this, a poor, blind person wearing a placard as he felt his way slowly down the street through a crowded throng. The placard had on it these words: "Pity the poor." Yes, the poor are to be pitied. But as I saw the consideration shown this man here and there, my mind took another turn, and I said: "Pity the prosperous for they are likely to be proud, and forgetful, and self-centered, and selfish and arrogant. Pity the prosperous!"

So when our prosperity comes, let us take it all to Christ. And we are to remember that He is interested in all that prosperity. He is interested in that young man starting his new business, and that other man whose business has already been splendidly launched, and that other who has brought his business to a great success. Jesus is interested in all legitimate business everywhere. Let us go and tell it all to Him.

Mark it, my friends, the day of testing will come, when everything will be submitted to the searching eye of Christ. Indeed, that day of testing is here right now. Well did our great President say that the world is on fire, and everything is in the crucible, everything is in the melting pot, everything is undergoing change. And we are to bring now all our successes and all our achievements to Jesus, that He may advise concerning them, even as He deems best.

There was a great business in another section of the land that was upborne when an awful time of testing came. One of the junior partners said afterwards: "The business never could have stood the time of awful testing which came but for the fact that our senior partner had great resources outside of the business, on which to draw, and he did draw on them freely and saved the day for our business." So is Christ our great Partner, and we can draw on Him, and ought to draw on Him. In the day of testing, or trial, or prosperity, or what not, we are to draw on that great Divine Partner, with his infinite resources and his measureless mercy. He would have us come and bare all our business before Him.

When else are we to go and tell Jesus? We are to tell Jesus when our day of pleasure and song and gladness has come. I wonder if there was ever any wedding quite so beautiful and holy as the wedding in Cana of Galilee, which Jesus attended. Jesus did not frown on their pleasures, you may be sure, on that happy wedding occasion. Jesus was no killjoy on that wedding occasion; nor is He ever a killjoy.

Oh, how glorious to have been there and to have seen Jesus as He stepped forward and greeted the bride and bridegroom when the wedding ceremony had been concluded! And how wonderful to have heard just what Jesus said to that happy bride and the man standing by her side, the man of her heart and love! Jesus did not frown on any worthy pleasures. Jesus was not and is not a killjoy for the deep, sweet pleasures of life. We are to bring them all to Him, and we are to say to Him: "Come Thou in all of our pleasures, and restrain us, and constrain us, that we may not go too far, that we may not miss the deep meaning of all these good things wherewith our lives are dowered and crowned."

45

When else are we to tell Jesus? We are to tell Jesus when the day of spiritual doubt comes. I wonder if that day does not come to us all, the day of real spiritual doubt. I was in a home recently where a tragic death had occurred and I was touched deeply by the comment one man made to another, as he said: "Last night a certain citizen was in this home. When he spoke concerning this sorrow he said: 'Oh, well, the grave will end it all, for there is nothing beyond. There is no God unto whom we must answer, no hereafter where we shall know the meaning of life's mysteries and share in the glories of its achievements and rewards. All is enclosed and covered out of sight to be heard of no more, when the clods cover the casket in the grave.' "

Oh, I trust there are not many like that! Spiritual doubt, though, comes in some measure to us all and some raise questions about God, the Father, and about Jesus and immortality! Others raise questions about heaven and hell and the Bible. Now what am I saying? When your spiritual doubt comes, you are to go and tell all that to Jesus. He is the Light of the world and He will know what to say to you. He is the great revealer of truth, and He will know what to reveal to you.

If you wanted an opinion about some serious disease, you would go to some skilled physician, who had made a study of that disease and the relation of materia medica to that disease. You would go to the right source for help. You would go to some diplomat, who could give you counsel, if you wanted it, on questions of government or statecraft. You would not go to some novice. You would not go to someone ignorant and uninformed. You would go to the best authority to be found. Now, when spiritual doubt comes, and questions come, take them all to Jesus and say: "O Jesus, Thou Saviour, Thou Light of the world, Thou Teacher, Thou Revealer of Truth, Thou Revealer of God, Thou Helper in the day of darkness, I bring my case to Thee. Shine upon me with Thine own light that I may have light."

All of us are subject to doubts. There have been times when the only prayer I could utter was: "Lord I believe. Help Thou mine unbelief." Oh, I took it all to Jesus and said: "Shine on this dark experience and give light and leading." And out of the perplexity, and out of the confusion, there came light and leading. Take your doubts to Jesus. O men and women who have doubts about religion, do not trifle with them! Take them all to Jesus. Probe them to the very depths. Do not trifle with them. You have too much at stake.

There is one other occasion, and that occasion should perhaps be stated first, before all else, when we should come to Jesus and tell our story to Him. We should come and tell the story of our needs to Jesus because of that fearful malady of moral sickness which has come to us all, the name of which sickness is sin. We should bring all that to Jesus, for no man has resources in himself sufficient to weather life's storm and to confront death and the great beyond, unafraid and unarmed. No man has the resources moral and sufficient within himself. Every man is under the blight and the touch of this moral sickness, the name of which is sin.

Every one has to come, therefore, candidly and honestly, not seeking to conceal the situation, but stating what the publican stated when he came: "God be merciful to me a sinner." Everyone should come and frankly say: "I confess my guilt, my loss, my lapse and failure. I acknowledge my dereliction, my weakness, and my dark chapters and mistakes. Lord Jesus, I can not work out my salvation by myself. I can not recover myself from my failure and loss and condemnation. So I come to Jesus, Saviour and Physician and Helper."

And when you come like that to Jesus He will say: "I will put your sins far from you, as far as the east is from the west. I will put them behind my back. I will cover them with my blood. You will hear of them no more if you will

47

bring your case to me, and trust your case only and utterly to me." Oh, how glorious, how glorious that we can bring our cases of need and lapse and moral sinfulness to Jesus!

Now, whatever the case, sorrow, perplexity, spiritual doubt, spiritual battle, spiritual struggle, spiritual failure, whatever the case, Jesus says: "Commit it all to me and I will be your Saviour and Master. I will be your Guide and Deliverer. I will be Righteousness and Power to you, even forevermore."

In a moment we shall sing a song which is a heart-felt prayer. I quote it for you:

> Pass me not, O gentle Saviour,
>   Hear my humble cry;
> While on others Thou art calling,
>   Do not pass me by.
>
> Let me at a throne of mercy
>   Find a sweet relief,
> Kneeling there in deep contrition,
>   Help my unbelief.
>
> Trusting only in Thy merit,
>   Would I seek Thy face;
> Heal my wounded, broken spirit,
>   Save me by Thy grace.
>
> Thou the spring of all my comfort,
>   More than life to me;
> Whom have I on earth beside Thee?
>   Whom in heav'n but Thee?

And as we sing this hymn, who is here who will say: "I have already found this great Saviour. I have already told Him of my trust. I have already told Him of my surrender. I have already told Him that I choose Him as my personal Saviour, gladly, unhesitatingly, wholeheartedly I have already told Him that. I would like to take my place with the church."

Or does someone say: "That is not my case. I have neglected my duty. I have gone into wanderings and into

48

backslidings, and into courses forbidden and evil. I am a backslidden Christian. I would like to come and renew my vows with Jesus. I would like, in the presence of all the people, to tell Him that I do come back. In His mercy and goodness He has spared me. I do come back." Come then!

Or does someone say: "That does not reach me. I have never made my surrender to Christ. I have thought about it. I have planned about it. I have pondered in my heart about it. I have meant to do it. But I have delayed. I now make my decision. I take Jesus at His word, when He says: 'Him that cometh unto me, I will in no wise cast out.' I take Him at His word and tonight I make my surrender to Christ, that He, from tonight, may be my Saviour and Master."

If you are here, come while we sing, and make your complete surrender to Him.

CHAPTER IV

Property Versus People

C H A P T E R   I V

Property Versus People

~~~~~~

> *And Jesus asked him, What is thy*
> *name? And he answered, saying, My*
> *name is Legion; for we are many.*
> —MARK 5:9.

THIS account from Mark is the most important account in all the New Testament of demoniacal possession. The subject is a very difficult one. One thing is certain, that it was a most aggravated form of Satanic influence, and in considering it we do well to remember that.

Light and darkness are always strongest when they are put side by side. When Jesus confronted this man face to face, when He came into direct contact with sin, however such sin was expressed, then was seen the light and darkness by reason of the contrast as it could not otherwise be seen when conditions were different. There are three or four suggestions in this story of the healing of the Gadarene demoniac, which this morning we may lay to heart with profit.

Here is one: The greatness of man. Horace Bushnell has a sermon you would do well to read on "The dignity of human nature as shown from its ruins." If you can find such sermon, be sure to read it. In that sermon he calls attention to the common argument of the greatness of a civilization as shown by the ruins that are left of such civilization. Through the generations that have gone, countries have risen and then have fallen, and the wrecks of their fall signify the greatness of their civilization in the day of their prosperity. By the ruin that has come to man, by the awful downfall that he has suffered, the great preacher discusses

53

the dignity of human nature. He shows how great, how wonderful man is by reason of the depths into which he has fallen from the marvelous heights to which he was elevated. Shakespeare, in speaking of the dignity of human nature, says, "What a mighty piece of work is man, how noble in reason, how infinite in faculties! In form and action how like an angel! In apprehension, how like a God!"

David had the same lofty conception when he said, "What is man that thou art mindful of him? For thou hast made him a little lower than the angels, and hast crowned him with glory and honor. Thou madest him to have dominion over the works of thy hands."

Now here is the picture of a man who was the camping place of six thousand devils, for a legion of devils was in him. Marvelous is the nature of man that it could be so. It suggests the amazing possibilities in man for good or for evil. Man's body is represented as being the temple of the Divine Spirit, and every Christian, every believer on Jesus, is himself the temple of the Spirit of God.

Here in one's body, in one's mind, in one's nature, may be the camping place for everything bad in all the earth. A legion of devils possessed this poor, unfortunate Gadarene, leading him whithersoever they chose. Surely here is a picture, both of the greatness and the weakness of man, that he should be the camping place of six thousand evil spirits from hell. What an awful revelation we have here, of man's greatness and weakness. Well may it excite our admiration, and well may it excite our alarm.

The power of Jesus Christ can reconstruct and save any man. There is not a more desperate case presented in the Bible of the havoc wrought by sin than the case of this demoniac. He was altogether helpless to direct his steps. He cried in the mountains; he dwelt in the tombs. No man could tame him. He had passed the restraint of the civil authorities; he had gone utterly to the bad; he was led by Satan captive absolutely at Satan's will. The man was impotent, utterly helpless. That was his awful condition.

But one day Jesus came into the section where lived that Gadarene demoniac. Jesus confronted him face to face. Instantly there was a conflict. The evil spirits in the poor man recognized the superiority of the Divine One, whom they were confronting. Quailing and cringing and frightened, they cried out, "Why hast thou come hither to torment us?" They were conscious, when they confronted Jesus, of the superiority of His divine nature, and cowering before Him, they had thus to cry out.

Here was One whom they knew had by a word calmed the storm-troubled sea. Here was One whom they knew had by a word multiplied the handful of loaves and fishes and fed the five thousand in the desert. Here was One who had touched His finger to the eyes of the blind, and they saw. He had given speech to the dumb and hearing to the deaf ear. He had cleansed the polluted body of the leper, and had given life to the pulseless body of the dead. Satan, the prince of demons, knew Jesus, and here a host of his evil spirits cowered before Jesus.

When Jesus meets an evil spirit there is always and instantly a conflict, and Jesus Christ is the victor every time. The poor abandoned woman of the streets was in His presence crying out her sense of guilt and shame and wreck, and in a moment she was sent away cleansed with the word that she sin no more. A robber died on the tree, after having spent his life in rebellion against God; but, dying, the robber's heart was melted into repentance and contrition and he was saved. The most brilliant persecutor of the Church of God, Saul of Tarsus, one day met Jesus on the Damascus road. Saul became Paul the Apostle, unmatched in all the tides of time as a preacher of the Gospel. When Jesus Christ takes hold of a case, He saves with His great salvation in every case, and henceforth in that life He is victor.

There is another striking suggestion in this story — a suggestion of the almost unlimited power of money. In almost every situation of life money plays a tremendous part. Here we see it issuing forth in this case before us. Jesus healed the demoniac, and drove out the legion of evil spirits and the man, clothed and in his right mind, went out to witness for Christ in his home and among his fellows. When the news spread that the untamed man, the wild man, the utterly wretched man, the man who was a terror to his country, had been cured by Christ a sensation was created.

Then there occurred one of the saddest of all the revelations in the Bible, one of the most deplorable revelations ever made by human nature. When the men of the community looked into the situation they found that the evil spirits had gone out of the man, and had been given permission to enter the swine, and that two thousand swine had rushed violently down the hill and plunged into the sea and were drowned. On the one hand was a bad man made good, a bad man tamed, a bad man reconstructed, a bad man saved, a human being ransomed and disenthralled from Satan's power; but on the other hand there was much loss — two thousand hogs — and the issue was joined. This was the issue: People versus Property. The men of Gadara said, "This must not go on. Though we have the object lesson before us, though we have the wild man tamed and made good, though we have Christ triumphant in the worst case we ever beheld, yet if this means that our citizens are to be saved at the expense of our hogs, then we will let our citizens go, for we value our hogs more than our people."

Is there a sadder revelation of the depth into which human nature can be plunged than that? Now we can believe the statement of Paul that, "The love of money is the root of every kind of evil."

Christ stood in the wildest community of New Testament days and met the greatest evil, the worst evil, in all New Testament stories; and Christ by a word vanquished Satan and made the worst man in the land happy and noble Yet the men of that community said, "If it is a question of saving men at the expense of our hogs, we will take the hogs and let the men go." Then they courteously but very strenuously insisted that Jesus leave their coasts. And of course he took them at their word and departed.

I know of nothing in all literature more awful, more horrible than this story. It is the awful revelation of the blinding, debauching power of money. Yes, yes, the love of money is the root of every kind of evil. It will blind men; it will debauch men; it will corrupt men; it will sear and emasculate man's noblest powers. If men master money, they are masters of one of the great forces by which the world may be lifted up. But if men are mastered by money, there is no slavery on earth more galling and ruinous than that. The men who bow down as devotees in some jungle in Africa to their little gods, made by human hands, are no more idolaters than the men in a Christian land controlled by the love of money.

Back of every attempt to sacrifice men for money is the Gadarene spirit. Back of every attempt to sacrifice men for money is the same spirit we find here in God's Word, written down for the warning of the world. That is the spirit that explains every improper advantage taken by one man over another. That is the spirit that explains every unsafe building which a man puts up to rent, when after a while its faulty construction may ruin its tenants. That is the spirit that explains every licensed evil in our land. It is the spirit that explains every improper rebate given by every corporation in the country. That is the spirit that explains the defiance of God's authority and the desecration of God's commandments everywhere. It is the love of money finding expression today, even as of old in the Gadarenes. It is the same spirit working today with the same awful results.

Oh brethren, I pray that this part of the message may claim your most earnest consideration. When Christ's people confront the world with the plain commandments of His Gospel, the same issue is met today. The world looks on

57

and smiles if we sing beautiful songs and pray beautiful prayers and prophesy beautiful things. But when the Gospel demands that men shall keep God's day, they answer, "We prefer hogs to God's day." Let the gospel demand that Christ's word, because it is the authoritative Word of God, must be obeyed, the Gadarene spirit at once finds expression and coldly says, "Will the Master please leave our coasts?" Oh this incident is one of the saddest revelations of the debauching power of money, that one ever meets.

Jesus took these men at their word and left their coasts. Ah! the tragedy of it! They said, "Please go," and He said, "I will go." That is what He does yet. A man may drive Jesus from his heart. "Behold I stand at the door and knock. If any man will open the door I will come in and sup with him and he with me." When the issue is joined and the man says, "Get thee away," Jesus takes the man at his word.

The wild man of Gadara, now healed, made a request of Jesus. Let us note what it was. It was a very natural request: that he might be with Jesus. You can understand why he wanted to be with Jesus. Oh, what a debt of gratitude the man owed to Jesus. He wanted to be a learner. He wanted to be with Jesus who had done so much for him. The man did not know whether or not these spirits would return and overpower him again, and fear made him wish to be with Jesus. But this was not Jesus' plan for the man. He said to the man, "Go back to thy home and tell thy friends what great things the Lord hath done for thee, how he hath had compassion on thee and saved thee."

In that commission is the commission for every saved man. Oh, how we wish at times to be with Christ, just to be with Him and forget all else. It was perfectly natural for Simon Peter yonder on the Mount of Transfiguration to say, "Lord, let us build here three tabernacles." Simon meant that they should just stay there and be happy. It was perfectly natural, but it was not Christ's wish. "Go back and tell others

58

what the Lord hath done for thee. Go back and be an evangelist for Christ. Go back and be a missionary for Christ." Christians are not saved simply to sit down and sing, but saved to go out and win others for Jesus Christ. The going church, the obedient church, means a present Saviour with us; while a disobedient and inactive church means the absence of Jesus from it.

But I will tell you a thing to keep in mind about it all. We may not here sit down and bask in blissful fellowship with Jesus as we shall do when we reach the heavenly home. But we may work for Him until the summons comes, and while working for Him we may have His spiritual presence with us, and that will illumine every path and will dispel every cloud and give peace to every heart. "Lo, I am with you all the days." So we may be with Jesus and at the same time be doing His work faithfully until the gates open and we are received to be with Him, face to face.

The same Saviour who cast the demons out of the man of Gadara, and cured him, and saved him, can do the same thing for men today. If there is one today, like the demoniac, held by the evil spirits of drink, of lust, or covetousness, or unbelief, or the love of money, or whatever the evil spirit, Jesus can break every shackle, and He will set you free the very hour you surrender to Him. Yes, He will save you now if you will let Him. You do not have to understand it all; you have only to submit yourself to Him, and His great work of forgiveness and salvation shall be done in your heart, without delay, and you shall today and forever be His and He yours. Burdened by sin, perplexed as you may be by doubts and fears, come to Jesus right now with the prayer, "Here Lord, I give myself to Thee, 'Tis all that I can do," and His own blessed word for it, He will not cast you away. Would you be saved? Then yield yourself completely and forever to Jesus, now while we pray.

CHAPTER V

When Jesus Rejoiced

CHAPTER V

When Jesus Rejoiced

In that hour Jesus rejoiced in spirit.
—LUKE 10:21.

JESUS is represented in the Bible as "a man of sorrows and acquainted with grief"; surely, He had occasion overwhelming for both sorrow and grief. "He came unto his own, and his own received him not." He was buffeted and despised; He was scorned and rejected; He was maltreated by those whom He sought to help. He came with mercy in His hands and they spat upon Him, trampled Him down and drove Him from their cities. And that went on until, in Gethsemane's garden, His heart was broken by the weight of the great sinfulness of the race, which great penalty He took upon Himself and paid for on Calvary's tree. He had every occasion to be "a man of sorrows and acquainted with grief."

And yet, there was a deep undertone of joy in the life of our Saviour, all the way along. While He wept, there was a deep undertone of gladness. While he sighed, there was also the thrill of joy. He looked ahead to the end; He visualized the last great harvest. He could view final results; He saw ultimate triumphs; He understood His Father's purposes, and He knew that those purposes were not to be thwarted, but would come to blessed fruition by and by. And though at times Jesus seemed overwhelmed with sadness and sorrow, yet there was a great undertone of song and of gladness. "Who, for the joy that was before him, endured the cross, despising the shame, and now is set down at the right hand of the throne of God."

But what is the particular occasion calling for this statement, "In that hour Jesus rejoiced in spirit!" What occasion, what circumstance called forth that expression? The scriptural lesson read a few moments ago brought out those cicumstances with clearness and with force. Christ had sent out "seventy others," in addition to the twelve apostles. He had sent them out on a tour of the nearby cities and the towns, and had given them specific directions as to their method of going and working. They went gladly, according to His divine commands. And, after a season, the seventy came back and made their report. They gave an account of their trip. They explained to the Lord something of the results of their labors; and this was what they said, "Master, even the very devils are subject to us, through thy name." One said, "I spoke and the sick man was healed." "And I spoke," said another, "and a demon was driven out." "And I spoke," said another, "and sickness was gone." They all rejoiced at their tremendous and triumphant success on this, their first great soul-saving tour under the command of Jesus. And when they told Him that even the devils were subject unto them, when in Christ's name they bade them depart out of men, Jesus, as if in musing, said, "I beheld Satan as lightning fall from heaven." And then the text goes on, "In that hour Jesus rejoiced in spirit."

Now, what are some of the manifest reasons for His joy on that occasion? Our scripture passage suggests them. Jesus rejoiced in spirit on that occasion because, for the first time, He beheld the ministries of an aggressive and consecrated group of His followers. Hitherto, only the twelve apostles were at work. Now, seventy others — so far as we know not one of them was a preacher, but laymen, plain, practical people — seventy laymen, so far as we can judge from scriptural teaching, went out on this great missionary tour for their Lord, two by two, just as the twelve apostles had gone. Here, there, and yonder they questioned, and witnessed, and testified, persuaded concerning the things of the kingdom of our Lord Jesus. Marvelous was their success. And so they came back with many trophies of the Lord's saving grace and made their report. It is no wonder that Jesus rejoiced!

At first it might have seemed that the apostles, the Twelve, were to have all the power and do all the evangelistic and missionary work of the kingdom of God. Doubtless the laymen among the many disciples of Jesus had been thinking that such work was not for them. Jesus had sent forth the Twelve and committed unto them great and marvelous power; and it seemed that other people were simply to stay at home and look on and be mere spectators in the great plan. But now "seventy others" were sent out. And when they returned, their report to the Lord was, "Oh Master, we had glorious success. People received us; they heard us; they believed our teaching; and even the devils, when we spoke using thy name, were driven out of demon-possessed people."

For the first time, then, our Lord looked upon the successful work of a group from the rank and file of His followers. Their success brought Him deep joy. It is a significant fact that whenever Christ's church has been content for her preachers to do all the work, that church has waned and declined in spiritual power. It is the divine plan that all the disciples of Jesus shall be His witnesses. The layman is as much called to be a witness for Jesus Christ as the preacher. In a sense, every saved soul is an ambassador for Jesus Christ. And our Lord looked that day upon seventy laymen who had gone out and thrust their sickles into the ripe, waving harvest fields, and had come back with exceeding joy and strength, and with many trophies for their Master. That was what made Him rejoice!

Look, my brethren, for a moment, at the history of the past, and behold how much it means for a layman to be active in the kingdom of God. Abraham, the father of the faithful, was a layman. Joseph, that mighty minister down in Egypt who was such a marvelous illustration of the

65

providence of God, was a layman. Caleb and Joshua, the brave men who went to spy out the promised land, and came back with their minority report, that they were able to overcome and drive out all the armed opposition against them — these men, too, were laymen. Gideon, who fought so valiantly in a time of Israel's sad decline, was a layman. Barak and Jephthah, who fought so valiantly on another occasion, were laymen. Samson, who astonished the lands with his superhuman might, was a layman. Mordecai, who behaved so gallantly at a still different time in Israel's sad decline, was a layman. Nehemiah, who thrilled the people with the great, and daring, and seemingly impossible project of rebuilding the walls of Jerusalem, was a layman. And in New Testament times, we find many examples of the influence and the power of laymen in the kingdom of God. Cornelius was a layman. Aquilla was a layman. Gaius was a layman. Stephen was a layman. Philip, for a while, was a layman. Many great and influential men in the New Testament churches were laymen. Their imprint is seen on the holy pages, and their power to bless has come down through the passing generations.

Our Lord rejoiced on that great occasion because He beheld that day a prophetic vision of the victories that would come to His churches down through the ages whenever their preachers and their laymen, working together, went forth with the life-giving message of the gospel of redeeming love which is centered in Him, the Saviour of the world. Jesus rejoiced with unspeakable joy as He beheld that vision.

The ideal of the kingdom of Jesus is that every man and woman, everyone saved by His grace, shall be a personal herald and witness for Jesus Christ. Everyone. "Would God all the Lord's people were prophets," was the great wish of Moses of old. And the New Testament ideal of a church is that every believer shall be a prophet, though not in the same sense. Every man is not called of God to stand in the pulpit and preach. But every saved man and woman is called of Almighty God to be a witness for Jesus Christ in his speech, his vocation, his position, to the last limit of his power, as much as I am called to preach. That is the divine ideal.

Oh, that we may come to this blessed and glorious ideal! Shall a man be a son and yet have no obligations to his father? Shall a man be a father and yet have no obligations to his child? Shall a man be a husband and yet have no obligations to his wife? Shall a man be a citizen and yet owe no obligations to his state? Shall a man be a Christian and yet owe no obligations to Jesus Christ? Oh, is Christianity just a badge to be worn? Is salvation merely a thing to be possessed? Does it not impose a solemn obligation upon the saved to put forth one's best efforts to win the lost to Christ Jesus, the one and only Saviour? Our Lord rejoiced because on that great occasion His people were measuring up to His divine plan.

And still again, Jesus rejoiced on that occasion because they went forth, when He bade them, with unquestioned obedience to His plain command. When He summoned the seventy around Him and outlined the task He had in mind for them and told them of the dangers, the difficulties, the sad situations in which they would find themselves at times, the men did not waver or hesitate. They went forth with glad, obedient, responsive hearts to His divine command. It is conclusive evidence today that one is a Christian when He desires to obey Christ and does obey Him.

Some years ago in a neighboring town where I went to preach, a railroad man was converted one night. He was a matter-of-fact fellow, accustomed to making decisions and making them quickly. The morning after his conversion he came to see me and said, "I have come to get my orders." That was new language to me and I said, "I don't understand; what do you mean?" He replied, "I am used to

67

obeying. Wires flash out to me several times a day telling me what to do. Last night I received the Son of God to be my Master. What are my orders? Sir, I don't know the Bible; I never read it. But I know I have surrendered to Him. What does He want me to do next?"

That is the spirit of Jesus Christ's true disciple; and I said, "The next thing is an open alignment with His church, an out-and-out placing of yourself on the Lord's side. This you can do by accepting baptism which Christ commanded because it is symbolic of His death, burial and resurrection, and the sign of the death and burial of the old man of sin and the resurrection of the new man in Christ Jesus to walk in newness of life." "Well," he said, "tell the preacher to give me a chance tonight and I will be baptized for I must leave on the train tomorrow morning and it will be some time before I am back." And just like that he took up his duties in the kingdom of God.

The followers of Jesus displayed great boldness. They went to all kinds of people, high and low, rich and poor, good and bad, saying, "In our Master's name we bring you a message, and you will do well to heed it today." And uncounted thousands, even in one generation, heeded the message of those friends of Jesus.

Have you read the story of John Knox's daughter, Jane Welch, who, when her husband was in prison for his fidelity to duty, went to the ruler to make a plea for her husband's life? The ruler said, "If your husband will cease his present activities I will release him." And she looked at the ruler and stretched out her apron and said, "Sir, I would have my husband's head, bleeding here in my apron, before I would have him go back on his duty." Hers was a magnificent tribute to duty. Oh that all Christ's friends would likewise magnify their duty to obey the commands of Christ to be His witnesses even unto the ends of the earth. Those seventy laymen whom Jesus sent out unhesitatingly obeyed

His commands. They performed their Christ-assigned task. They did their duty. The results were glorious.

And then Jesus rejoiced because of their success. When the seventy returned and made their report, Jesus said, "I saw Satan as lightning fall from heaven." It was a vision to Christ of the ultimate triumph of the gospel — a vision of Christ's ultimate triumph everywhere as the Saviour of men. He saw a great day coming when Satan should be bruised under the heel of the marching triumph of the Son of God.

Sometimes the question is asked: Do missions pay? The answer to that question is a mighty "Yes." This earth has no record comparable to the reports made by Christ's missionaries since the birth of modern missions when William Carey went out to India. Not even the story of the spread of Christianity during the first three centuries of the Christian era is so thrilling as the saga of modern missions during the past century and a half. Obedience to the great Commission of Jesus pays in every way — commercially, scientifically, morally, socially, spiritually, redemptively. Yes, missions pay a thousand-fold. No doubt many of the triumphs of modern missions fill the heart of Jesus with joy as did the success of the seventy laymen.

Jesus rejoiced that day because He beheld their joy. They came back and said, "Master, we are very happy. We had a great time. Sick people were healed when we called upon them; devil-possessed people were delivered from their demons; and lonely-hearted ones were made glad when we told them about Thee. Oh, Master, we had a great time!" It made Jesus glad to see their joy in His service. Serving Christ and obeying Him brings us the greatest joy in all this earth. "If you love me, keep my commandments," is His oft-repeated injunction. Let us in this church fill His heart with joy because of our obedience to His commandment. Then, indeed, will we know the joy of our salvation.

My ambition is that our church shall be, from center to circumference, a missionary church. Every true church of the Lord Jesus Christ must be both evangelistic and missionary in principle and practice. And therefore my highest ambition for this blessed church is that every member, from the oldest and the wealthiest to the youngest and the poorest, shall be deeply interested in the salvation of the lost to the remotest bounds of earth.

A recent letter from one of our missionaries in Japan says, "Our missionaries over here pray for you time and time again, because you pray for us." And another from China says, "We missionaries get together and pray for the First Baptist Church in Dallas, because you people pray for us and uphold us, and are holding up our hands." Such expressions fill our hearts with rejoicing and should encourage us to do far more than we have ever done for our noble missionaries and the blessed work they do in obedience to Christ's commands.

The labors of the seventy brought great rejoicing to the heart of Jesus. And we can add to His rejoicing if we will be personal soul-winners and also be informed, loyal, prayerful, generous supporters of world-wide missions. God grant that every member of our blessed church may be possessed of a heart which is twenty-five thousand miles in circumference in its interest, its prayers and its sacrificial giving. Let us this very day bring rejoicing to the heart of our Saviour and Lord, as we lay at His feet our gifts for the cause of world-missions. Let us do this cheerfully, generously, even sacrificially, for His sake.

CHAPTER VI

Hindered Prayers

C H A P T E R   V I

Hindered Prayers

〜〜〜〜〜〜〜〜〜〜〜〜〜〜〜〜〜〜〜〜〜〜〜〜〜〜〜〜〜〜〜〜

That your prayers be not hindered.
—I PETER 3:7.

THE Apostle Peter, in one of his epistles, uses this suggestive expression: "That your prayers be not hindered." There is, then, such a thing as hindering one's prayers. It is a matter to which attention is earnestly called all through the Bible. We sometimes hear the expression in a public prayer, "We thank God that we are yet on praying grounds with Him." It is an expression that is no doubt used care lessly many times. To be able in spirit and in truth to use such expression is to be very near to God and to have the life most graciously surrendered to His will. There is no such thing as effectual, prevailing prayer otherwise. The careless, worldly, unsubmissive Christian cannot successfully pray. For him who would prevail in prayer, this is the great law ever to be kept in mind, as stated by the Master: "If ye abide in me, and my words abide in you, ye shall ask what ye will, and it shall be done unto you."

As in the natural world the delicate, subtle workings of electricity may be hindered by influences very slight, so much more in the spiritual world, prayer is hindered and spiritual blessings are withheld, because of a too careless consideration of the great laws that obtain in the kingdom of God.

Among the many hindrances to prayer a few may here be named.

Prominent among these is a wrong motive. The Apostle James thus expresses it: "Ye ask, and receive not, because ye ask amiss, that ye may consume it upon your pleasures."

73

This strikes at the heart of the matter. But one motive is to actuate us when we offer supplications to God, and that motive is His glory. All other motives are vain. Christ is to be all and in all. His will is to be the supreme consideration. When we come, therefore, to order our cause before God we are ever to put to our secret souls the searching inquiry, What motive actuates this prayer? Whatever the object sought, whether a gracious revival in our church and community, or a deeper work of grace in the individual heart, or the salvation of the souls of our own loved ones or strangers, the glory of God is to be kept in view continually and supremely.

Closely connected with the foregoing hindrance is this one: lack of submission to the will of God. Prayer is sometimes very anxiously and fervently offered, but in its last analysis the will of God is not submitted to. As the Master thus prayed in Gethsemane, so must all His disciples pray: "Nevertheless, not as I will, but as thou wilt."

By submission is not meant a stoical feeling something like this, "Oh, well, God will do what is right about it and I will give myself no concern." Yes, God will assuredly do what is right, but will you? David praying for the restoration of his child is an illustration in point. For weary days and nights he prayed on incessantly, but when the message reached him that his child was dead he quietly submitted to the will of God as it was now revealed unto him, and went on uncomplainingly about his work. For aught he knew the life of his child was dependent upon his supplications, and he prayed on till he knew God's will and then he yielded to that will. We are to pray as though all depended upon our poor supplications, and at the same time to trust all to the direction and blessing of God without whom we can do nothing. There is evidently a vast amount of stoical indifference here, foolishly supposed to be prayer to God and submission to His will, but which is as far from true prayer and true submission as is the east from the west.

Lack of definiteness is another grave hindrance to much of our praying. Oh, the vagueness, the indefiniteness, the scattering and wandering and rambling of many of our prayers! Nearly everything in general is mentioned to God, but not one thing in particular is He asked to do. Such a petition, sent to a legislature or to congress, would be thrown into the waste basket. Let us tell God just what we mean and what we wish. Let us be specific and personal as was Abraham when he prayed for Ishmael, "O that Ishmael might live before thee." If we mean Ishmael when we pray, then let us say Ishmael.

Another most serious hindrance to prayer is unforgiveness in the heart. In the model prayer given us by the Saviour, one of the things to be daily prayed is, "forgive us our sins as we have forgiven those that sin against us." The Revised Version brings out this thought with startling distinctness. If we may expect God to forgive us our sins against Him, then, certainly, we are to forgive our poor, sinful brothers who sin against us.

Sin cherished in the heart hinders prayer most grievously. On this point David says, "If I regard iniquity in my heart, the Lord will not hear me." For God to hear and answer and bless the suppliant whose life is careless, worldly and consciously in willing alignment with sin, would be to compromise the Almighty and deny His holy character. Therefore appropriate was the prayer of backslidden David, "Restore unto me the joy of thy salvation; and uphold me with thy free Spirit: then will I teach transgressors thy ways, and sinners shall be converted unto thee." We wonder many times why the heavens above us seem as brass and no response comes to our earnest prayers. Doubtless, this statement in Isaiah is frequently the explanation: "Behold, the Lord's hand is not shortened, that it cannot save; neither his ear heavy, that he cannot hear; but your iniquities have separated between you and your God, and your sins have hid his face from you, that he will not hear."

We talk about "set times" for the Lord to work through His people in His kingdom. His time to work is always when His people are in blessed harmony with Him. Obedience to the plan He revealed to Solomon would mean unceasing spiritual prosperity and enlargement for His people. This it was: "If my people, which are called by my name, shall humble themselves, and pray, and seek my face, and turn from their wicked ways, then will I hear from heaven, and will forgive their sin, and will heal their land."

Then, again, our prayers lack earnestness. How dare we presume to talk to God if our hearts be not in the matter? Even men will not stop to hear us if we do not have a message. Turn to God's book and see the men who had power with God and consequently had power with men. They were men of desperate earnestness in prayer. What more awful earnestness was ever seen than that of Moses praying for backslidden Israel? Hear him as he offers his prayer to God: "Oh, this people have sinned a great sin, and have made them gods of gold! Yet now, if thou wilt forgive their sin —; and if not, blot me, I pray thee, out of thy book which thou hast written." What a desperate, urgent, awful prayer!

Look again at Jacob wrestling at Jabbok in view of the looked-for crisis of tomorrow. He was utterly at the end of his own strength. God alone was his help now, and all night long Jacob wrestled in prayer, girded by this conquering resolution: "I will not let thee go, except thou bless me." All heaven was pleased with such awful earnestness, and to Jacob came the answer: "Thy name shall be called no more Jacob, but Israel; for as a prince thou hast prevailed." Oh, if ever we are to be candid and urgent and earnest, let it be so when we pray!

In connection with such earnestness we are to be importunate; that is to say, we are to keep on till we have God's answer. It is so easy for us to weary in well-doing, and especially to weary in prayer. Surely, this ought not so to be, in the face of our Lord's exhortations and promises. When thus tempted to be weary in prayer, let us call to mind Christ's story of the importunate widow at last winning her case before the indifferent judge; or His illustration of the friend pleading with his neighbor for bread at the midnight hour, and winning because he wouldn't quit. So much do we lose because we cease our prayers. "I say unto you, Ask, and it shall be given; seek, and ye shall find; knock, and it shall be opened unto you."

Perhaps the greatest of all the hindrances to successful prayer is lack of faith. We cannot mightily win in the spiritual world if we do not mightily believe. God is to be implicitly believed and His words literally accepted by His people. This is the condition of the Lord's doing great things for His people. "If thou canst believe, all things are possible to him that believeth." When in the flesh, with a certain people, Christ could not do many mighty works because of their unbelief. All through His Word He begs His people just to take Him at His word, to put Him in remembrance of what He has promised, to try Him and prove Him. And of us today He might say just as He said of unbelieving Israel, "How long will it be ere ye believe me?" If we only believed God as we ought, what might we not accomplish? Do not our inmost hearts send up the cry, "Lord increase our faith"?

It does not need here to be argued that all prayer is to be offered in the name of Christ. "Whatsoever ye shall ask the Father in my name He will give it you." How infinitely far does God seem from us if Christ be taken away! In Him we have a daysman through whom we may approach the Father. "For there is one God, and one mediator between

77

God and men, the man Christ Jesus." None of us have ever yet scaled the heights or sounded the depths of the meaning of the little expression so often spoken in our prayers — "for Jesus' sake."

What is your chief hindrance when you approach the mercy seat? Is it that the answer God sends may be consumed upon your own pleasure? Is it that you wish your will and not God's to be done? Is it that you have nothing definite to mention to God? Is it some cankering unforgiveness in the heart? Is it some cherished idol sinful in God's sight? Is it that your heart is indifferent and lacks earnestness? Is it that the delayed answer makes you faint-hearted and weary? Is it that you do not believe what God says? What is your main hindrance in prayer? Have you earnestly sought to be delivered from it? "My God shall supply all your needs according to His riches in glory by Christ Jesus." "If any of you lack wisdom let him ask of God, that giveth to all men liberally, and upbraideth not, and it shall be given him."

Holy Father, teach us how to pray! This we ask above all things else, help us to pray just as we ought! We would ask it for Jesus' sake!

CHAPTER VII

A Question of Profit and Loss

CHAPTER VII

A Question of Profit and Loss

～～～～～～～～～～～～～～～～～～～～～～～～～～～～

*What shall it profit a man, if he shall
gain the whole world, and lose his own
soul?*
—MARK 8:36.

THOSE who read the Bible — and certainly every
man and woman should read the Bible every day, whatever
else you may or may not do — those who read the Bible
do not read it long without making the discovery that the
Bible is the book which calls our attention to the big questions, the eternally important questions. Many of these
questions are searchingly personal and others of them are
social questions, touching upon our relations to other people.

Take, for example, the very first question in the Bible:
"Where art thou?" This question is searchingly personal
and very soon thereafter you come upon the question searchingly social: "Where is Abel, thy brother?" We are bound
up together in the big bundle of life. If anybody in the
world goes wrong and you and I could have by any means
prevented it, God tells us he will require his blood at our
hands.

As we turn through the Bible, other questions stand out
like mountain peaks: "Is thine heart right?" Why does that
matter? It matters everything, because out of the heart are
the issues of life. Then this question confronts you: "What
is your life?" Further on we come upon Job's question:
"If a man die, shall he live again?"

We will take as the question for our meditation today that
remarkably familiar question asked by Jesus: "What shall

81

it profit a man if he shall gain the whole world and lose his own soul?"

If a man should gain the whole world, so that over it he could write: "This is mine," and do so at the loss of his soul, the transaction would be an infinitely tragic failure. Supreme things are often lost by inattention. Business, well-ordered for a season, again and again later along goes on the rocks because of inattention. Too much was taken for granted in the administration of the business. Care was not sufficiently exercised in guarding every point in the development and conservation of the business. A man is wise in the realm of business if he will look carefully and frequently to the conditions of his business, and himself have detailed knowledge about it, no matter how many his workmen, or how much they may be trusted. Supreme things often are missed and lost through inattention.

Now, here the Master sets before us supreme things, and sets them in contrast, and asks this question of the ages: "What shall it profit a man, if he shall gain the whole world, and lose his own soul?" The case is stated as strongly as language can put it. You will note the two objects set in contrast — the world and a human soul.

Look first at the world. Jesus states it just as strongly as it can be stated — "If he shall gain the whole world." Imagination cannot measure the world's resources, its materials, its wealth, its mighty means. We are utterly confounded as we try to comprehend the vastness, the richness, the wondrousness of the resources of this world. A small part of it, if one shall own it, shall make its possessor inexpressibly wealthy, speaking after the fashion of men. If one should own this small city, he would be counted the possessor of marvelous wealth. If one should own a tithe of the resources of this city, what a wealthy man he would be, speaking after the fashion of men! If one owned this imperial State, what a wealthy man he would be! If he owned this fair nation, what a Croesus in wealth he would be! If he owned one particular product of the world, all of that product, how wealthy such a man would be! But the Master states the case for us just as strongly and broadly as it can be stated: "If he shall gain the whole world."

Nobody ever has gained it. Several men have tried to do so. Alexander tried it, and thought he had gained it, and stood there weeping by India's seashore, because he thought there were no other worlds for him to conquer. And yet there were other lands even at that time, unexplored, and other peoples, unknown to Alexander. He had conquered only a small portion of the world. Napoleon sought to master Europe and he made many conquests. What a titanic man, what a Colossus was he! He terrified great countries and small countries alike! He went from one military achievement to another, until at last it looked as though he was going to bring Britain under his rule and sway! But he had his Waterloo. A self-centered man always has his Waterloo. The day comes to king, or Kaiser, or emperor, or ruler — proud man, mighty man, whoever he is — self-centered, when he shall go down "unwept, unhonored, and unsung." These and other men tried to gain the world, but failed. If they had gained it, if any human being were to gain it, the world would not satisfy. We are prone to seek things which we imagine will satisfy the human heart, and yet if we had them in all their vastness, richness and plenitude, still would we be utterly dissatisfied. Take material wealth. How men expend their brains, their wills, their intellects, their keenest judgments, their imaginations, their energies, all their powers, in the accumulation of material wealth! And yet, if one should get it all so that every piece of property on all this planet should be owned by one, it would fail utterly to satisfy.

Croesus got a great portion of it. Fabulously wealthy was he. So wealthy was he that with his wealth he could buy a vast kingdom, and then would have enough left to buy still another vast kingdom. But his wealth did not satisfy him. Do you recall his exclamation when he came down to die? Piteously he wailed out the expression, again and again: "O Solon! Solon! Solon!" And when the watchers by him asked him what he meant, he said: "Solon told me that though my money did not satisfy me while I was living, when I came to die it would satisfy me, and I am crying to him to tell him that I am more miserable now, dying, than ever before." He had vast wealth but died like a dog in the ditch. And if a man should get all the banks, and all the ranches, and all the properties, and all the mines, and all the material resources that are to be had on this planet, still he would be utterly unsatisfied.

Again, full many a time men chase after that thing called fame — that transient, evanescent, unsatisfying thing, called fame. But when men get it for a season, how it gets away! The man about whom the crowd says, "Hosanna!" today, is likely tomorrow to have it cry in his ears, "Crucify him!" How fickle, how unsubstantial, how fleeting, how unsatisfactory is all the fame, all the popularity, all the honor, that earth can give!

And then, full many a time people spend their lives in running the round which is called "human pleasures." Solomon tried it to its last fearful finish. And what a tragedy was much of his life! Everything that could appeal to the physical senses was tried by this man, who began so well, but whose head was turned, and whose heart was so wretchedly spoiled by human emoluments and honors and blessings which were accorded him.

And when at the last he had sipped at all the fountains, and had inhaled the perfume of all the flowers, he cried out with a pessimism never excelled in human speech: "Vanity of vanities, all is vanity!" Said he, "I have tried it all, and all under the sun is but weariness to my flesh." That is the world with God left out. That is the world at its very best.

That is the world with all it can give, and all that it has; all that it can marshal, to fortify, and reinforce, and inspire, and gladden. The world at its best will not, can not satisfy an immortal soul!

The world does not satisfy, because it does not last. We need to remember that. One of the tragedies, indeed, the supreme tragedy of human life, is that often when a man thinks he is ready to live, he must die. The most fitting symbol of human life is that of the broken shaft. Even when a man has his wits about him, and thinks he is sound in judgment, discerning and careful, he is stricken with paralysis or apoplexy, and hurried away, shambling down through the Valley of the Shadow. So that if a man could get possession of all the world, what would it amount to in view of the fact that he could have it only for a brief day? There is but a step between us and death. The stoutest, heartiest, bravest, most valiant man in all this world has only one short step between him and death. Suppose he had the world, what would he do with it, with a space of such brief duration as that?

What is your life? It is like a vapor that appeareth for a little time, and then vanisheth away. It is like the mist of the morning, dissolved and broken by the mighty sun. What is your life? It is like that swift-passing ship. Do you see it? There it is! But how quickly it dips beyond the horizon! What is your life? It is like the grass, which groweth up in the morning, but in the evening it is cut down and withereth. What is your life? Swifter is it than the eagle on his flight. So that if you got the world, all its wealth, and all its honor, and all its pleasure, just at the time when you were gloating over them you would be hurried down the way of dusty death.

Then what are you going to do when you come to the swelling of the Jordan? When the real you leaves the old body in which your spirit has lived for sixty or seventy years, or forty or thirty, or more or less, and you go down into the Valley of the Shadow, what are you going to do then with all your money and material resources? You will do just what one of the greatest financiers in the East did awhile ago. His name placed on the wires would put the financial world into a quiver but when he came to that last day he sent for a friend, a man of God, a glorious preacher, and when the preacher went into his room at eventide the mighty financier said, "I wish to be alone with this preacher." And then, as they were alone there, the minister said to him, "What is it you wish, Mr. Vanderbilt?" And he said, "Oh, Mr. Deems, I want you to sing a song for me, and then I want you to pray, for I am dying tonight." The minister said, "What do you want me to sing, Mr. Vanderbilt?" And Mr. Vanderbilt said, "Sing that song:

> *Come, ye sinners, poor and needy,*
> *Weak and helpless, sick and sore;*
> *Jesus ready stands to save thee,*
> *Full of pity, love and power.*

"Sing me that. I am a poor sinner at the very best, and I need help from above." Not a word about his railroads; not a word about his stocks and bonds; not a word now about the things human and earthly. He was sinking into the grave, and he needed more than earth could give him.

Another one of the great financiers of our nation was asked awhile ago, "Aren't you exceedingly happy?" And he said, "Happy about what?" "Happy because you have so much wealth." He said, "All I get out of it is my board and clothing, and endless worry. That is all I get out of it."

The poet was right:

> *This world can never give*
> *The bliss for which men sigh.*
> *'Tis not the whole of life to live,*
> *Nor all of death to die.*

Beyond this vale of tears
There is a life above,
.Unmeasured by the flight of years;
And all that life is love.

There is a death whose pang
Outlasts man's fleeting breath.
Oh, what eternal horrors hang
Around man's second death!

Suppose some man could grasp the world in his arms and gloat over the fact that he was its possessor, what do you think he would do when he met God at the judgment throne? Every one of us must meet Him there. Whatever events the future has for us, here is an inescapable event. Every human being will stand yonder before God's throne of judgment, and we shall there answer for the deeds done in the body. We shall answer for the use and the abuse of every privilege in life. We shall answer for the way we have lived year by year, and hour by hour, and moment by moment. We shall answer for the words spoken by our lips, for the secrets cherished in our hearts. We shall answer for everything, public, and secret, that may attach in any way to us. What would a man do there with the world on his back, if he could carry it there, without God? Oh, the tragedy of a human life without God!

My attention was called by one of our distinguished citizens yesterday to two great citizens in another city, whom we both knew. He said that the ghastly thing about it was that they lived without God and that they put the stamp of their influence on every young man in all that city. As we spoke of those men and commented on how they had lived, and how they had died, we shuddered to think of the wide swath of influence they had cut through that long generation. I knew them both. I had preached to them both. I had done my best, my little best, for them both. I had seen them grow white-haired and stoop-shouldered. I had seen the years pass on, until their years, because of the infirmity of age, made their lives practically an intolerable burden. They touched thousands of lives, and put only the touch of materialism on those lives. Oh, the suicide of it! The tragedy of it! No man has a right to exert that kind of baleful influence on others. No man has the moral right to occupy a position in the occupancy of which some other man may hide or get hurt. No man has that right. Since every man must choose his own way, let him look about him and say, "Since I must live my life, I will live it in a way not to harm a human being by the power of my example. I will seek to help rather than hurt all who may follow me."

That is one side of it. Now, Jesus said, "What shall it profit a man, if he shall gain the whole world, *and lose his own soul?*" Over against the world Jesus sets a human soul. And He asks, where comes in the profit, whatever your gain, even though it be the loftiest that the human imagination can conceive, if you make all that great gain at the loss of your soul. The value of the soul cannot possibly be estimated adequately. But that it is of surpassing value in God's sight is quite evident. If we look at what the soul has cost God — your soul and mine — something of its value will begin to dawn upon us. God so loved you that He separated Christ from His heart and sent Him to earth, to be a man, to be born of a woman, to live under the law, to keep the law, and to suffer for you and die for you. God thought that much of a human soul. "The Son of God, who loved me and gave Himself for me," is the way the Scripture speaks of the death of Jesus Christ for sinners. Oh, that sacrifice!

You will think a soul is of vast worth if you will seriously reflect upon Jesus those thirty and three years He was here. You will think a soul is of great worth if you watch Jesus during the three marvelous years of His public ministry, and see how, by precept and example, He sought to point men in the upward way. You will think a soul is of worth if you go where you can watch the echoes of the Master's prayer in Gethsemane's shadows that fearful night, when He cried, "O my Father, if it be possible, let this cup pass from me. Nevertheless, not my will, but thine be done." You will think a soul is valuable if you can see Jesus after they have stripped Him and laid upon His back forty stripes save one; and again, as you see Him go forth to Golgotha's hill bearing His own cross, until at last He faints from weariness and loss of blood under that burden. You will think a soul is valuable if you watch Him there, and realize that it is all for you. You will think a soul is of surpassing value, if with your mind and heart you see Him there, as they nail Him to that accursed cross, and lift it up, and leave Him there to die that cruel death for you — you will think a soul is valuable.

"Father, forgive them; they know not what they do," was a petition He made for you and me, as well as for the men about Him, as He hung on that cross, and there made atonement for your sin and mine.

If the soul of man had not been of infinite value, God would never have permitted such a sacrifice as that for a human soul. The redemption of the soul is the most costly transaction earth ever saw. It cost the suffering, the shame, the death of the Son of God, that the human soul might not die forever. Surely, that soul is of infinite worth which could necessitate such an outpouring of Love Divine.

And then, you will see its value if you will consider for a moment the capabilities of a human soul. Oh, who can measure the capabilities of a human soul? That soul was made in the image of God, and though such soul is fallen and marred, covered with the muck and mire of earth, yet such soul has a marvelous relation to its Almighty Creator. I do not wonder that Shakespeare, the greatest dramatist of the centuries, said, "What a mighty piece of work is man! How noble in reason! How infinite in faculties! In form and movement, how like an angel! In apprehension, how like a

God!" Oh, the capacities of a human soul. That human soul, tonight wallowing yonder in the gutter, made bestial by sin, is worth more than the material universe, because of the capacities of such soul.

Will you think about how much a soul can know, how much you and I are to know? When we have been in the house of life yonder ten thousand years, we shall still be pupils, and Christ, the Divine Master, will Himself be teaching us. There will come a time when the least man in this room, the least informed man, shall know more than the world combined shall know this side of the grave. One soul, the least of all, shall progress higher in the endless eternities than the whole world knows this side of the grave. Oh, the capacities of the human soul!

There is another truth about the soul of which I desire to remind you. The soul is to live forever. Solemn, even terrible thought, that the soul is to live forever! The soul of that little baby, born yonder in the modest cottage or in the palace today, is to live when the stars and the moon and the sun have all been rolled away. It is to live forever! And that tramp, beating his way from door to door in our city, his soul is to live on forever. And that abandoned wreck of humanity is to live on forever and ever. What capacities does a human soul have!

And then there is another thing for us to remember. When the soul is finally lost, it is an entire loss. When Francis the First was defeated at the famous battle of Pavia, crying like a child, he said to his men, "My men, we have lost here today all except honor." When men have not lost their honor, they can go on and on. When they have not lost their honor, they can rise up and face the foe. But when the soul is lost, it is a total loss. When the soul is finally lost, it is a loss without any compensations. There are compensations for many human and earthly losses. For example, there was a great fire in Chicago, some years ago, and a hundred thousand people were turned out of house and home before the flames could be quenched; but the outcome was that better buildings and sanitary quarters were made in that section of squalor and wretchedness and frightful poverty and dreadful disease, so that out of the fearful loss there came compensations of great value. Long years before there was a fire in London, one of the greatest fires in human history, and it seemed that the great world-city was utterly doomed. Yet out of that holocaust came better buildings and sanitary conditions. London took on new hope and new health, physical, mental and moral, because of the rehabilitation of the wastes occasioned by that great fire. There are losses which have within them great compensations. But the loss of a soul is a loss without any compensations. If a man die in his sins, unanchored to Jesus, the sinner's Saviour, his is a loss without compensations.

Finally, and most tragic of all, if a man's soul be finally lost, then the loss is irreparable. If the soul be lost finally, it is an eternal loss. Some losses can be repaired. A man may lose his health, and by dint of patience and perseverance he may recover it and be a strong man again. It is often so. A man may lose his property yet he may gather his powers and concentrate his energies and recover it and more. A man may lose his position in the realm of human honor. Some enemy, some foe, some opponent may drive him to the wall, and yet he may summon his powers and to-morrow recoup all his losses and carry his flag to a higher pinnacle than ever before. But when a man goes out into eternity unanchored to Christ, the soul is lost, irreparably and eternally.

I should like to ask you this question: Are you giving your soul a chance? You must be the judge. No man can answer for you. Each man must answer for himself. Judas sold Jesus for thirty pieces of silver, about fifteen dollars in our money, and went the way of eternal waste. He is called "the son of perdition," which means "the son of waste." Hell is the land where men have lost out forever. What are you doing that your soul may live and prosper? O my friend, let Christ save your soul! You cannot save it. If you could, He would not have come, and Calvary would not have been necessary. Let Christ be your Saviour. Do you hear His voice? "Today, if ye hear my voice, harden not your heart." Do you feel miserably guilty because of your sins? Then hear Him say, "Though your sins be as scarlet, I will make them as white as snow." Do you feel that your weaknesses are many and pitiful? Let that not deter you, for Jesus says, "He that cometh to me, I will in no wise cast out." O my fellow-men, how are you treating your souls? Let us bow our heads and ask the all-wise God to make us wise enough to realize that the whole world is as nought compared with the salvation of the soul through Christ Jesus, our Lord.

CHAPTER VIII

A Prayer for Mercy

CHAPTER VIII

A Prayer for Mercy

~~~~~~

Jesus, thou son of David, have mercy on me.
—MARK 10:47.

IN EVERY congregation, probably at every service, there are assembled men and women who are in very deep, even desperate need of God. It is brought to my attention week after week, by personal conference and by letters through the mail, how near some come to take the ill-fated step toward their own utter destruction, yet who are providentially led to this house of prayer and hear and heed God's call. I say that week after week my attention is called to such, who come in desperate need of God. They come, sometimes, with that prayer which Job voiced when he realized that there was only One who could suffice him in the multitude of troubles which came upon him, and exclaimed, "Oh, that I knew where I might find him."

Now, to the man or woman who wants God's help, the Bible speaks exceedingly gracious words. God is a seeking God; the Bible represents Him everywhere as looking for people who want to find Him. God is more concerned that your case be right with Him than you are to have it made right, no matter how intense and even desperate is your longing to be right with God. In view of that certain fact, when men come to the house of prayer and hear God's call sounding in their ears and hearts, there ought to be no delay, no hesitation, no indecision; but there ought to be definite and positive surrender of the life to the Lord. I wonder if I am speaking to some who want the favor of God, who

have in some measure the sense that He is their Supreme
Being, who have had it burned in upon them that without
Him they are in danger of shipwreck for time and eternity.
Oh, how I would like to help you!

Let me read for you the account of one who came to Jesus
and had His blessing, and went away triumphant and rejoicing:

And it came to pass, that as he was come nigh unto
Jericho, a certain blind man sat by the way side begging:
And hearing the multitude pass by, he asked what it
meant. And they told him, that Jesus of Nazareth passeth
by. And he cried, saying, Jesus, thou son of David, have
mercy on me. And they which went before rebuked him,
that he should hold his peace: but he cried so much the
more, Thou son of David, have mercy on me. And Jesus
stood, and commanded him to be brought unto him: and
when he was come near, he asked him, Saying, What wilt
thou that I shall do unto thee? And he said, Lord, that
I may receive my sight. And Jesus said unto him, Receive
thy sight: thy faith hath saved thee. And immediately
he received his sight, and followed him, glorifying God:
and all the people, when they saw it, gave praise unto
God.

There is the picture of a man in desperate need who came
to Jesus with an earnest appeal for help and went away
with his request granted, with his sight restored and with his
heart swept with great joy. Oh, that the scene which I have
just read from Luke's gospel might be duplicated in this
place tonight! The outlines of that story are perfectly plain.
For a few minutes let us focus our attention upon them.

We have here the picture of a man sorely needing Jesus'
help. He was blind. What a pathetic affliction is blindness!
I have thought that no other privation was so poignant as
to have the sense of sight taken away. What helplessness

and pathos ever go along with blindness. Here is a blind man and you can imagine him soliloquizing, as he feels his way along the roadside and as he passes to one side of the road and listens to the tramping of the travelers who pass him. You can imagine him soliloquizing as he hears a crowd coming, and asking, just as blind people do ask, "Who comes there — who is it that passes by?" They told him, "Jesus of Nazareth passeth by."

He had heard that name before — Jesus of Nazareth, and what wondrous stories were connected with that name! Jesus of Nazareth — He had cured blind people; He had made the deaf to hear and the dumb to talk; He it was who, with a word, rebuked sicknesses, and caused the afflicted to take up their beds and walk; even the winds and the sea obeyed His voice! Jesus of Nazareth! "At last my time has come," the blind man said to himself, "At last my opportunity is here and I must make the most of it." So he cried without delay for the help of that great, delivering Saviour. He realized his need and he voiced it without hesitation or delay.

I wonder, as I hold up this picture out of the gospel story, if men and women have come to this place of public worship today who realize their need of God. If you think you can get on without Him, just as long as you think that, you will not have Him. If you think that your condition is not urgent enough, precarious enough, dangerous enough to call for God's help, then you will go on without His help. Those to whom God reveals Himself are those who are conscious of their need of His help. Oh, soul, I would help you if I may, to realize your need of God. Why were you made? What if you shall turn aside and frustrate the great plan of your Maker for you? You can do that. The highest dignity allowed you is the dignity of choice. You can say "Yes" to the gracious Saviour who comes, offering to bless you eternally; or you can say "No." With you rests the great matter of choice, of decision with respect to the proffered mercy of the divine Saviour.

Oh, if I could help you to realize your need of His mercy. What if you should live your life clear down to the end without His forgiveness, and without His guidance, and without His wisdom and without obedience on your part to His holy will? Then you would be a cumberer of the ground; then you would violate the high purpose God has for you; then you would come short of the divine program for your life. If, alas, you should die as you are, without reconciliation to God, without His transforming power in your life to fit you to meet Him unafraid and in peace; what then? You know the answer. It is doom, death, eternal separation from God and all that is good; and that is hell.

Now, this blind Bartimaeus, on the Jericho Road nineteen centuries ago, realized his need of the great Saviour's help and just as soon as he had opportunity to make his appeal to that same Saviour, he made it without hesitation and without delay. You will notice how he came with his appeal to Jesus. He voiced it in prayer. When they told him who it was that passed by, he cried out in a moment, without delay, "Jesus, Thou Son of David, have mercy on me." He voiced his need in prayer.

Oh, my friends, do you know what it is to pray? You are missing a supreme opportunity of life if you do not pray. You are running ten thousand risks if you fail to pray. You are facing perils and pitfalls more tragic than I can voice in words if you neglect to pray. Oh, my friend, would you pray tonight? Prayer is the sanest thing in all the world. God commands all men to call on Him. God tells us that if any man lack wisdom — that is the one thing every man and woman does lack, — "if any of you lack wisdom," let such a one "ask of God, that giveth to all men liberally and upbraideth not, and it shall be given him." Do you know how to pray? Have you tried to pray? Do you desire to pray? Would you have God's mercy and help as the blind man of old sought it for himself? Then, like the blind man of old, you are to voice your cry, "Jesus, Thou Son of David, the appointed Messiah, the long-promised Saviour and helper, I make my cry to Thee. Have mercy on me." That is prayer. It does not need to be long; it does not have to be eloquent; it may be broken and stammering; it may be voiced with words simple and few. But if with sincere heart you call on God, "Jesus, Son of God, Saviour of men, Divine Helper, without whose help men will make shipwreck of their lives, Jesus, I cry to Thee, have mercy on me"; if you cry sincerely, if you cry honestly, if you cry out of a heart fixed on following God, you are certain to have His answer.

This man prayed. The publican of old prayed. He and the Pharisee, you recall, went up to the Temple and prayed; and the Pharisee stood and talked with himself and the Lord was not pleased with his talk. But the publican, a sinner, who had sinned against law and sinned against order and sinned against himself and sinned against others, would not so much as lift up his eyes to Heaven, so conscious was he of his miserable failure, and his needs. He would not lift up his eyes to Heaven, but smote upon his breast, simply saying, "God be merciful to me a sinner." Jesus said, "I tell you, this man went down to his house justified rather than the Pharisee," who made his prayer and did not mean it. Oh, do you know how to pray?

This blind man prayed. Then he refused to be turned aside by difficulties that were put in his way to keep him from Christ. When he cried out to Jesus for divine help, the multitude rebuked him and reprimanded him, saying, "Don't repeat that. Jesus of Nazareth does not have time for a beggar like you; hold your peace." And when the crowd interfered and sought to block his going to Jesus, the blind man cried out so much the more, "Jesus, Thou Son of

David, have mercy on me." With his whole heart he sought
Christ. Hindrances could not stop him, difficulties did not
block his effort. With his whole heart he sought Christ. Oh,
the man who seeks the Lord with his whole heart will not
come short of the Divine mercy.

Is your heart fixed, my fellowman, my gentle sister? Do
you want God's help above all else? Do you want God's
help enough to refuse to be turned aside by any voice, however seductive and insistent? The heart which seeks God
like that finds God. The Bible tells us: "In the day that
thou seekest me with thy whole heart, I will be found of
thee." *"With thy whole heart."* Oh, men or women, wrong
with God, in need of God, come with your whole heart and
say, "As for me, come what may, hindered from this quarter
or the other, as the case may be, oh, God, my heart seeks
Thee, definitely and whole-heartedly, until Thou dost speak
mercy and peace to me." Come like that and the hour is at
hand when you shall have His mercy and His word, "Go in
peace. I have heard thee and I will bless thee." This is the
first lesson from this incident: Bartimaeus sought Jesus in
the right way.

And what was Jesus' response? When the blind man's
cry reached the ears of Jesus, though the crowd sought to
stop him from reaching Jesus, the record here tells us that
Jesus commanded that this seeker should be brought to Him.
Jesus was on His last journey to Jerusalem where He would
be crucified. He had a great mission to accomplish. Already
the shadow of the cross lay heavy across His heart. Yet when
this cry for mercy reached His ears, though the crowd sought
to drown it, Jesus stopped and said, "Bring that man to me."

Now the issue was joined squarely between Jesus and the
blind man. Will you look at it? Jesus asked him the point-
blank question, "What wilt thou that I shall do unto thee?"
In other words, "Be clear, be definite, be specific! What is
it now that you want of me? What would you have at my
hands? What is included in that cry on your part that I

100

shall show thee mercy? Tell me what you want me to do for you." And the blind man answered, "Lord, that I may receive my sight." You see he knew to whom he made his appeal.

Now if tonight Jesus stood on this platform, Oh, my fellow-sinner, hurrying with me to the judgment bar of God and to the eternity to come, suppose Jesus stood here on this platform and said, "What do you men and women want of me tonight?" Would you say, "I want to be forgiven of my sins, I want to have a power within me that will enable me to walk in the upward way according to Thy will"? Would you say to Him, "Be merciful to me, a sinner"? "Thou alone canst save. I trust in Thee."

Then to you He would say, like He said to Bartimaeus of old, "Thy faith hath saved thee. Go in peace." And as you went, your soul would know the peace of God that passeth all understanding, your heart would be flooded with joy and you would be able to sing:

> My hope is built on nothing less
> Than Jesus' blood and righteousness;
> I dare not trust the sweetest frame,
> But wholly lean on Jesus' name.
> On Christ, the solid rock, I stand;
> All other ground is sinking sand.

Blessed be God, Jesus will forgive and will change and will deliver, and will lift up and put your feet upon the solid rock if you honestly surrender to Him.

There is one more word. This blind man came to the crisis hour for himself. This was his last chance. Jesus never passed that way again. He was even then going toward His cross and one week thereafter He was nailed on that cross. The blind man had reached his crisis hour — it was then or never. Opportunity comes and pauses, but not long does it pause; it passes on and does not return. That same opportunity passes; it does not come back at all. This was the last opportunity Bartimaeus had to make his cry in person to Jesus of Nazareth for mercy. It was his crisis hour.

Solemnly, faithfully, prayerfully, I raise the question, Can this be the crisis hour for some of you? I cannot say. God knows about that; and it may be that your heart not only tells you of your own need but also tells you that Jesus Christ, the one and only Saviour, can meet your deepest need; that He is able to save to the uttermost them that would come unto God by Him. In that case, it is indeed a crisis hour for you. Jesus is here ready to save you, if you are ready to let Him be your Saviour. It is a time of golden opportunity for each one of you who needs and deeply desires the forgiving and saving mercy of the blessed Saviour.

If you are willing to have it so, you can, in this very hour, be forgiven and cleansed of your sins, if you penitently confess them unto God; you can be eternally saved by trusting fully in the Lord Jesus Christ; you can be guaranteed divine grace, help, comfort and love for time and eternity if you will here and now fully surrender to Christ and confess Him publicly as your Saviour and Lord.

Many and gracious are the divine invitations for you to do that. Hear and heed some of them!

Seek ye the Lord while he may be found; call ye upon him while he is near.

Whosoever therefore shall confess me before men, him will I confess also before my Father which is in heaven.

Come unto me, all ye that labour and are heavy laden, and I will give you rest.

Him that cometh to me I will in no wise cast out.

Will you come to Him now? Will you confess Him now? Will you seek Him while He may be found and call upon Him while He is near? If yours is a prayer for mercy — a prayer for pardon, peace and power, then come as we sing our hymn of invitation: "Jesus is Tenderly Calling."

102

CHAPTER IX

The Sinner's Path to God

CHAPTER IX

The Sinner's Path to God

I acknowledged my transgressions.
—PSALMS 51:3.

EVEN boys and girls will understand that this big word "transgression" means sin. It is a larger word than sin, but it means the same thing. So the speaker says: "I acknowledge my sins." The three hardest words in all the world to say, as they ought to be said, are these: "I have sinned." And yet to say them and to feel them rightly lies at the very foundation of a sinner's coming to God, so far as the sinner is concerned. The very first step in a sinner's coming to God is the recognition by that sinner of the awful fact that he is, in God's sight, a sinner. If he be not a sinner, then he has no need of a Saviour. An indispensable qualification for us to be saved is the recognition of our condition in God's sight, that we are sinners. Jesus said: "I came not to call the righteous, but sinners, to repentance." And again: "They that are whole have no need of the physician, but they that are sick." And again: "The Son of Man is come to seek and to save that which was lost." Would you recognize, then, the painfully solemn fact that you are a sinner in God's sight? If you will, and will come to Him rightly confessing unto Him your sins, then shall you be saved.

Be not deceived about the fact that you are a sinner and separated from God by your sin. There are two plain causes for such deception. One is that man is ignorant of the condition of his own heart. Upon that fact God says that "The heart is deceitful above all things and desperately

105

wicked: Who can know it?" Alas, how deceitful the heart is! Yet, at the same time, if a man will soberly consider how he treats God, he will be driven to the conviction of his own sad, sinful condition in God's sight.

Just consider how man treats God. God is his Maker. God is his bountiful preserver. God is the bestower of gifts and mercies and blessings beyond measure to man, and yet that man will turn his back on God, and seek to put Him out of his thoughts, and reject His counsels and His mercy, and make of no effect, so far as he can, the death of Jesus Christ. Oh, does a man need any other proof that he is a sinner, than just this, the way that he treats God? Receiving from God, as he does, countless and constant mercies, dependent upon God, as he is, for every breath that he draws, does he need any other proof that he is a sinner, does he need any other proof of his awful condition in God's sight than this — that he is willing to go one day, one hour, one minute, out of harmony with the will of God?

We must bring men back to the recognition of their personal relation to God. God is not a football to be kicked about by man. God is not some unworthy and ignoble being, to be ignored by man. God is man's Maker, man's Preserver, man's Saviour, man's Judge. Men must see the awfulness of their own sin, if only they will stop for a few moments to consider how they treat God.

God's Word is the standard by which our conduct and our character and our opinions are all to be judged. His Word is the one, supreme standard. Whatever may be our opinions, they are all to be discarded if they are contrary to God's Word. Now, when we come to God's Word, from beginning to end we read of man's lost condition by reason of sin. What saith the Scriptures? "All we like sheep have gone astray." "For there is no difference, for all have sinned and come short of the glory of God." "Except ye repent ye shall all likewise perish." "Verily, verily, I say unto thee, Except a man be born again he cannot see the kingdom of God." And these solemn statements could be multiplied indefinitely.

These scriptures are the end of all debate on this solemn matter. So, whatever may be your notions; whatever may be your sense of safety; whatever may be your opinion of your condition; know that the end of all controversy is reached when God makes His pronouncement upon your case. And God's pronouncement is that outside of Jesus Christ, the most amiable, the most moral, the most lovable man by nature is without God, and without Christ, and without life, and without heaven and without hope, and without salvation and without excuse and without escape. O sinner, let God's Word speak to you.

In God's sight, outside of Jesus Christ we are all condemned sinners, alienated from God, neither ready to live nor to die. Outside of Jesus Christ that awful doom is pronounced upon us by God Himself. I would have you recognize it and lay it to heart before it is forever too late. If we confess our sins as we ought, then there is mercy for us; there is salvation for us; there is eternal life for us.

But there is both a wrong way to acknowledge sin, and a right way. I do not believe there lives anywhere a man who does not sometimes confess his sins. Exigencies of life come upon him — things perplexing and distressing to his heart sorely try him — and in such hour he makes confession of sin. But, I say, there is a right way and a wrong way for us to confess sin. A man may confess sin and make his case worse. A man may so confess sin as to mock God.

Then, it is infinitely important that we seek the right way to confess sin. God gives us examples in His Book of men who confessed their sins, some to no profit, others to profit. Now, let us look at some of these examples.

Out of the Old Testament Scriptures there comes the tragic story of a man, who, in an hour of great stress, acknowledged his sins. That man was King Pharoah, down in Egypt. He confessed his sins in an hour of great stress, and yet he made his case worse after such confession. You recall the occasion of such confession. Long had he ruled oppressively over God's people, Israel, down in Egypt. They were Pharaoh's slaves, and were cruelly afflicted by task-masters, and their groanings came up into the ears of the all-wise, all-pitying God. God heard their cry and sent Moses, their leader, straightway to Pharaoh, the King, with the message that the King should let the people go out of Egypt into the land God had provided for them. The King defiantly challenged God. Matters went from bad to worse, until at last God said, in effect: "The King in Egypt shall surely know that there is a God to be reckoned with in the affairs of men, and that this God may not be trifled with forever with impunity." And you remember that one plague after another fell in swift succession upon that land. At last, God's death-dealing angel went through all the Egyptian borders, and the first-born of every Egyptian household lay dead in one night. Then it was that Pharaoh's heart melted, and then it was that his proud spirit relented, and then it was that he came to Moses, with confession of sin, and said: "Go, with your people, and serve your God, as ye have said, and bless me also."

Then the clouds of God's just judgments were lifted and Moses started with the people to the Promised Land. After they had gone, Pharaoh took back his confession and his vow. Pharaoh summoned his hosts again, and sent them with swift dispatch after the retreating Israelites. Pharaoh said substantially, "Overtake them. Recapture them. Bring them back. They shall be my vassals again, whatever Moses' God may say or do." Moses, with his hosts, had reached the Red Sea, as the hosts of Pharaoh followed in hot and relentless pursuit. Then God wrought a miracle for the help of His people, and the hosts of Moses crossed the sea dry-shod, while the hosts of Pharaoh madly followed on, only to be drowned in the depths of that sea.

Pharaoh is a type of man to be found in every community where the gospel is faithfully preached. He is the man who, in stress of sorrow or trouble or danger, confesses his sins, and when such stress has passed, he takes it all back. He is the man who, in an hour of great trial makes a vow unto God but when the trial is passed, withdraws the vow. He is the type of man who, in some hour of danger, makes a resolution in heaven's sight, and when the danger is over, takes it all back. He is the type of man who enters into covenant with Almighty God in an hour when his soul trembles with the deep sense of his need of God's help, but who, a little later, puts off the supreme matter of being reconciled to God until another time. He is a type of man to be found, probably, in every community.

There comes to my recollection, even now as I speak, the case of a man a few years ago who followed in the steps of Pharaoh. His wife was a devoted member of the church, a noble follower of Christ. One evening as the pastor was ready to dismiss the mid-week prayer-meeting, there came hurriedly into the meeting one of the community's esteemed Christian physicians. He said, "Pastor, don't dismiss them; wait a moment." The pastor and the people waited, and the physician came rapidly forward and said, "Mr. So-and-so, (calling him by name), is lying at the very gates of death. All of you know him and his devoted wife. Five physicians have just had a consultation about him, and so far as any human help is concerned, this man has already passed beyond the reach of materia medica, and there is no hope for him. But," said the doctor, "I believe in God." Happy thing when a doctor does; blessed is it for him and happy is it for his community. Sad thing it is when the opposite is true. "I believe in God," said he, "and I believe that the Great Physician may tonight rebuke the sickness. I want you to pray to that end. I have come from his bedside, hurriedly. I told him the situation. He is a man who has long put God out of his thoughts. He is a man who has lived for self.

109

He faces the situation now. I have told him that from the human viewpoint there is no hope, but I have told him we would take his case to God. And he bade me to hurry here to tell the preacher and the people that he wanted them to pray for him on just one ground, that God might spare his life in order that he might give his heart to God, and give himself, unstintedly to God's service."

The preacher said, "Personally I can pray for him, and in view of his statement, I can pray for him with much hopefulness." They all then prayed. It was a time of intense prayer. Then the people went their ways, and the very next morning the physician said, "The tides have turned; he will live; his improvement is marvelous, it is nothing short of Divine intervention to give a dying, condemned sinner another chance."

Thirty days thereafter the man was sound and well, on the streets, mingling with his fellows. One after another of those Christians went to see him, and looked him in the face, and said, "O friend and neighbor, wondrous was God's mercy to you to spare you. You will not delay now about surrendering your life to God, will you?" Would you believe it? He sought to evade their plea! The preacher said, calling him by name, "Why, sir, God has spared you in answer to prayer; what do you mean to do about your promise?" And the man said, with a shrug of the shoulders, "I was in a close place then; I had to do something; I had to make a great promise. But I will put the matter off for awhile. Some of these days, before I get in as close a place as that again, I will pray, and I will make my case right with God." The preacher protested. But the man went his way. And in that man's case it came true, just as the Scriptures so solemnly declare: "He that being often reproved, hardeneth his neck shall suddenly be destroyed, and that without remedy."

Some days later, as this man was leaving for another city, he was suddenly stricken with apoplexy and died without ever regaining consciousness.

There is no wisdom in any sane man's coming to life's end like that. There is no wisdom in treating God like that. It was the most desperate piece of presumption of which man can be capable. But that type of sinning may be found in nearly every community.

I speak, it may be, to some man here today who is even now living over this story in many of its sad essentials. One day, it may be, you came in from your work, and your wife met you with face pale and anxious, as she said with a sob, "O husband, the baby is the sickest I have ever known him to be. O husband, I was afraid he would not live until you got home. I called the doctor, yes. He is in here now. O husband, the baby is hard by the very gates of death." You went in, and glanced at the child, and then you went out alone as quickly as you could, and there behind the house, or in some other quiet place where no eye saw but One, you got down on your knees before God and said, "Great God, I am a sinner; spare my child and Thou shalt have me; let this awful disaster pass and I will be Thine." And God turned back the disease and the little child lived. But you have strangled to death that promise that you made in heaven's sight. O men, do your hearts respond to this solemn truth? Does it reach your case? Then know that yours is not the right way whereby a man should make confession of his sin to God.

The most difficult man in this wide world to reach with the gospel is the undecided man, the wavering man, the halting man. In every community, men hear the gospel under some earnest preacher, and it commends itself, not only to their judgment, but it grips their consciences, and they know in their heart's depths that he is speaking the things that are worthy of all acceptation. And they say, "We will give it attention." And yet they go out and deal in subterfuges, and apply to their consciences spiritual opiates, until at last their souls have little or no responsiveness at all to the call of the gospel of the Son of God. Have you not seen the picture of men dallying with the gospel as they hear it, fighting it off, resisting its great claims and its mighty impressions, putting them all away?

The most sensitive vegetable that grows, they tell us, is the little plant called the "sensitive plant," which responds in every tendril and leaf and fiber when it is touched, like the vibrations of some finely-stringed instrument. You may touch such plant again, and it will respond, but less. And again you may touch it and it will respond, but less and less with each succeeding touch. At last, no matter how rudely the little plant may be touched, its every tendril and leaf hangs flabby and unresponsive. The plant has at last been touched to death. Some men are like that. They are touched by God's truth and fight it off and drown it out and put it away, until at last, though the terrors of the judgment, though the eternity of hell, though the glories of heaven, though the expiatory sufferings on the cross of the infinite Saviour are all poured out by lips swept by the power of God's Spirit, yet they sound as an idle tale and men listen to it all with unconcern. When you trifle with your religious impressions you are taking the most desperate risk it is possible for the human soul to take.

I bring to your attention another man who made a confession. Judas confessed his sins. His was the confession of a man in utter despair. Judas betrayed his Lord for thirty pieces of silver, and then came back and said to the chief priests: "Let us undo our bargain. The money you gave me burns my hands and it burns my pockets and it burns my conscience and it burns my soul. Let us undo that thing." And they laughed him to scorn, of course, and then the poor wretch went out and by his own hands took his own life. He did it saying, "I have sinned, in that I have betrayed the innocent blood."

And that leads me to say that if there were no other reason why I would reject every species of infidelity in the world, when I see how unbelievers die I would reject every one of their theories. I have infinitely better reasons, however, for being a Christian, than seeing how men die. But I have seen men die, time and again, the saved and the lost, and I have heard their last expressions as their feet went into the cold stream; and if there were no other reason, when I see how an unbeliever dies; how he goes down into death's cold stream and out to meet God; when I see the consternation on his face, and hear the expressions that escape his lips, I would be driven utterly from every theory of unbelief and skepticism in the world.

But I turn from the sad lines of thought we have been pursuing. There is a right way for a man to acknowledge his sins which, when followed, means to be saved with the everlasting salvation. What case in the Bible illustrates that? Here is one. The prodigal son illustrates it. And the publican illustrates it. Others in the holy Scriptures illustrate it. But let us take the prodigal son. He confessed his sins and did it in the right way, and the outcome was that he came back to his father's house. Every one recalls his case. He was a restless, wayward, impetuous boy, wishing to get away from the restraints of home, and he went away over the protests of his father, taking his part of the estate. He went from bad to worse, until at last his goods were all wasted and his substance all expended in riotous living, and he came down to the depths of poverty and shame. And down there in that degradation and in that ditch of sorrow the young fellow began to think. Significant is that Bible expression: "He came to himself." And when he "came to himself" he said, "Why, I can do far better than this, at father's house, even as one of the servants. I think, too, how wretchedly I have treated father. It all comes back to me now. I will go back to father and say to him: Father,

113

I have sinned against heaven, and before thee, and am no more worthy to be called thy son: make me as one of thy hired servants."

There was the beginning of genuine repentance for sin. Simply being sorry for sin is not enough. Repentance, true repentance, is the turning away from that sin. The man who says, "I have gone in the evil way. I have disobeyed God and dishonored Him, but I will not keep it up. I will now turn. By the grace of God I will follow the Saviour," and does it, that is repentance.

Now see the prodigal as he comes home. Yonder he comes, ragged and weary, disgraced in his own sight; all broken in spirit. Yonder he comes, and as he approaches the old home you can almost hear his thoughts: "I wonder just what father will say and do. I certainly have no claims upon him, but I am going to say to him what is in my heart. I will pour it all out if ever I see him again." And while the young fellow goes trudging along, there is an old man away in the distance, looking down the road. And you can hear the old man's thoughts: "Oh, if son would only come back! Oh, if I could see that lad again! Dear, restless fellow, but still my boy!" And as the father looks down the road, he sees somebody coming, and you can again hear him think: "If that were just my boy, oh, if that were just my boy coming back!" And as the boy comes nearer, you can hear the old man think louder: "Upon my soul, he walks like son." And as he comes nearer, the old man's heart beats faster and the Scriptures say: "When he was yet a great way off," when the son was yet a great way off, "his father saw him, and had compassion, and ran, and fell on his neck, and kissed him." "When he was yet a great way off." And you can see them as they come together. You can hear the boy as he says: "Father, I have sinned. I do not ask again to be your boy, father. I must tell you how I feel, before you and in heaven's sight." But the old man hugs the ragged son to his heart and kisses him again and again, and

114

calls out to the servants: "Bring forth the best robe and put it on him. Put a ring on his hand and shoes on his feet. Kill the fatted calf. Start the music. The boy that was lost is found. The boy that was dead is alive." What is all that about, my friends? It is a picture of how much God wants to save a poor, wandering, lost sinner. And it is also an example of the right way for a sinner to repent of his sins and confess his sins and cast himself on God's pardoning and saving mercy.

Oh, sinner, do you want to be saved? Your path to God is the way of true repentance for sin and sincere faith in the Lord Jesus Christ, the only Saviour. He is able to save unto the uttermost them that would draw near unto God. No matter what your past may have been, if you, here and now, will truly repent of your sins and in faith will accept and confess Jesus Christ as your Saviour and Lord, your future, your eternal future, will be filled with peace and joy and victory such as you have never known. This is especially true if you will faithfully follow Him the rest of the way.

Do you believe that Jesus Christ is able to save you? Do you believe that He wants to save you? Are you willing for Him to save you now? If so, He invites you, and I invite you, to walk down one of those aisles and take me by the hand and tell me that you come as a poor, needy sinner, trusting in Jesus to forgive you and cleanse you and save you. Come as this great company stands to sing:

> Just as I am, without one plea,
> But that Thy blood was shed for me.

CHAPTER X

Thy Will Be Done

CHAPTER X

Thy Will Be Done

~~~~~~

> *Thy will be done in earth, as it is in heaven.*
>
> —MATTHEW 6:10.

LET US think together for a little while on the most important prayer that we are called to pray here in our earthly life. This prayer is indicated for us in one terse sentence, spoken by Jesus in the incomparable prayer which He has given as a model for His people. We speak of this prayer often as "The Lord's Prayer." Perhaps it might more properly be called "The Model Prayer," "The Pattern Prayer," or "The Disciples' Prayer."

One day when Jesus was here in the flesh, He gave himself to a season of prayer, and one who saw Him and heard Him was so moved that he made the request, "Lord, teach us to pray as John also taught his disciples." At that time Jesus gave in abbreviated form the prayer which Matthew recorded in fuller form as part of the Sermon on the Mount. Who on earth knows how to pray this prayer like it ought to be prayed? We probably run over it in memory oft times without much reverent thought at all.

> *Our Father who art in heaven, hallowed be thy name, Thy kingdom come. Thy will be done in earth, as it is in heaven. Give us this day our daily bread. And forgive us our trespasses, as we forgive those who trespass against us. And lead us not into temptation, but deliver us from evil: For thine is the kingdom, and the power, and the glory, forever. Amen.*

Oh, who can scale the heights and sound the depths of that model prayer? There is one sentence in the prayer which indicates the most important prayer for us to pray: "Thy will be done in earth, as it is in heaven." The loftiest privilege of human life is to do the will of God. No other duty is so high as that. No other privilege is so glorious as that — to do the will of God. God has a will and man also has a will. It is the will of God to rule over us. All nature, except human nature, obeys the will of God. There is one discordant voice to be heard in the world and that voice is man's. He disobeys the will of God. We know that evil is here by man's will, by man's choice. The basic sin of all is selfishness. It was back of the sin of disobedience in the Garden of Eden. Evil is here by man's choice. We can say "yes" or "no." Man said "no" in the beginning to God's will, so evil is here by man's choice, by man's preference.

Now what is the meaning of this great prayer? "Thy will be done in earth, as it is in heaven." The meaning in a sentence is for us to pray that God may have His way with us here in this world even as He does with the hosts who are in the heavenly world.

This prayer for the doing of God's will comes before our prayer for daily bread. Mark it again. "Our Father who art in heaven, hallowed be thy name. Thy kingdom come. Thy will be done in earth, as it is in heaven." Then comes our prayer for daily bread. "Give us this day our daily bread." Note the order! Does not that order terribly rebuke us? Are not many of our prayers distressingly selfish? How often do we pray for the will of God to be done on earth before we pray that we may prosper in business; that we may be healed from sickness; that we may be recovered in health? How often do we follow this order? "Thy kingdom come, thy will, O Father, be done here on earth as it is now done in heaven above." How often do we pray that, before we come down to our daily necessities, to our problems of food and raiment, to our daily work and burden-bearing and general welfare? Does not this order terribly rebuke us?

You ask, "Shall we not pray about our daily bread?" Yes, certainly! "And shall we not pray as we go about our business?" Yes, of course! The more you pray about it, the better it will be for you and for your business too. "Shall we not pray about our health when it is undermined, about our bodies when they are sick?" To be sure! Make it a matter of earnest prayer. Pray about health. Pray about business. Pray about the daily adventure, the daily work, the daily burden-bearing, but let it be in the proper perspective. Let it come in its proper order. More important than our daily bread is it for God's kingdom to come on earth. More important than that we shall have food and raiment in gracious measure is it that God's will be done here on earth as it is done in heaven above. More important than that our sick bodies shall be cured, is it that God's kingdom shall come and His will shall be translated into life in our city, state, and world.

Therefore, we are to call ourselves back to this primary, transcendent, supremely important prayer and let it come in the order in which Jesus placed it for us. It may be God's will for us to be sick for awhile. Very well, His will be done. It may be His will for us to travel the dark, rough way of adversity for awhile instead of the way of prosperity. Very well, His will be done. Hezekiah traveled the road of adversity and in talking to the Lord about adversity said, "O, Lord, by these things men live." Martin Luther testified that his greatest teachers of all were teachers of adversity. Oh, if out of the economic depression and disquietude and unrest and disappointment and broken plans, the people shall be nearer to God, God's will be done!

What a challenge this prayer is to us! "Thy will be done." Whatever it is; wherever it leads; whatever it costs; whatever it means! Thy will be done. If it means a season of trial, of adversity, of pain, of suffering, of fear — very well, Father, Thy will be done. If it means broken plans, blasted prospects, faded hopes and disappointed expectations, Thy will

121

be done. Oh, it is a challenge, the most difficult challenge that the soul ever faced. To pray this prayer without evasion or reservation is a real test of Christian character. Do you pray it? Have you prayed it today? Can you pray it without any reservations? "Father, Thy will be done, with me and my family and all my programs and plans and interests; Thy will be done." Can you pray that prayer?

I confess frankly, in my early Christian life I held back from praying this prayer. There never was a prayer in all the world that so frightened me as this prayer. Never another prayer that so terrorized my soul as this prayer: "Thy will be done, whatever it is, for me and mine." If I know my heart now, if I understand my poor self, I would not dare pray any other prayer that was contrary to the prayer which says, "Father, Thy will be done with me and mine, whether by life or death, Thy will be done!"

It will help us to remember two things as we try to pray this prayer: First, whose will is it we want done? It is not the will of a tyrant, not the will of an enemy. It is the will of the best friend we have in the universe. It is the will of our Heavenly Father, the one who created us; the one who keeps us; the one who crowns us with every mercy and grace and goodness. He is our Father who sees ahead and loves and cares and provides, our Heavenly Father. We need not be afraid of Him! No, never afraid.

In peace will I both lay me down and sleep;
for Thou, Lord, alone maketh me dwell in safety.

His will is the will of love. The love of God is more tender than the love of the best mother for her little child who nestles in her arms and sleeps on her heart.

And then, second, this other word: Let us remember His will is always best for us, whatever it is. God's will for us is not only right because it is God's will, but it is best, for He dealeth with us from the standpoint of mercy and grace and love. His will is always best.

You may say, "There is much about it that I do not understand." Certainly. We walk by faith, not by sight. Oh, how difficult for us to walk by faith! The highest tribute to the Heavenly Father is for us to walk by faith. The chiefest education that the human spirit gets in this world is in walking by faith and not by sight. Where we cannot trace God, then are we to trust Him. When we walk by faith we say, as Job said when all the lights had gone out for him; when all his defenses seemed broken down; when all hope seemed gone, "Though He slay me, yet will I trust in Him."

Stonewall Jackson, great Christian soldier, wounded accidentally by one of his own men, dying at the battle of Chancellorsville, said; "If I live it will be for the best; if I die it will be for the best. God knows and directs all things for the best for His children. God's will be done." That is exactly the way to pray.

I am thinking of a little woman long afflicted but who had marvelous faith in the eternal verities of religion. Oh, how pitiful was her physical condition. One day, realizing her serious affliction and with ever deepening sympathy, her aunt who cared for her said to her, "My dear niece, if the Lord Jesus were to ask you today to choose whether you would go on to heaven and be taken out of this world of suffering, or whether you would stay here a while longer, you would have no trouble in making your choice, would you, dear?" She waited a moment and said, "I would ask Jesus to decide it for me, for I would not know which was the better for me." And that is exactly the thing for us to say. I would ask Him to decide it for me, whether I should get out of all this tribulation and suffering and pain and go to the House of Life and Light and Love with all the limitations of earth left behind me forever, or whether I should learn some more lessons and get some more discipline — some more of walking by faith and not by sight. We are not to be afraid to pray this prayer.

There is another truth that should be emphasized. This is a prayer, not only for those who are tested and who suffer and who are distraught and over-burdened and tried in the work and experience of life, but this prayer is a call for the strong, for the heroic, for the able-bodied. This prayer is a call for cooperation with God. Thy will be done: Not talked about; not submitted to; not resigned to. Thy will be done. Father, thy will be translated into the life of America and throughout the world. Thy will be done here on earth as it is done in Heaven. It is a call for cooperation with God. A great call! We are fellow-workers with Christ. Are there duties which we should perform for God? Then, we become His fellow-workers if we get under the yoke with Him and go about translating into life the will of God. Are there wrong conditions about us which ought to be changed? Then, with God's help, and according to His will, it behooves us to devote our highest energies to bringing about the needed changes. In other words, if we pray, "Thy will be done," we must, to the limit of our power, seek to answer our own prayer.

Years ago, there was a dreadful scourge of typhoid fever in England and the Christian people asked the Prime Minister to appoint a day of prayer that this scourge might be stayed. He said, "I will gladly do so. But more than that, I will ask all the scientists to get busy and see what it is that causes this scourge of sickness which pervades old England from border to border."

Let us pray and let us also seek to rectify wrong conditions. I knew a whole family in my boyhood that went through a dreadful siege of malarial fevers. For months the awful battle went on. One would go down with it as another got well. Bye and bye the old country doctor said, "There is some local cause. Let's see what there is about this house that has caused all this trouble." And then he looked carefully and there under the house was a cellar filled with long-standing water. He said, "Let this cellar be completely cleaned out, be utterly renovated or this sickness will persist with increasing severity." When the source of infection was removed the scourge was ended. We are not simply to pray. We are to answer our own prayers to the limit of our powers. If we can, we are to put hands and tongue and feet and purses and loyal service with our prayers or else our prayers may be futile.

That was a great story about some neighbors who met to pray for their neighbor, a widow whose husband had left her with a house full of children and with very little to eat and with very little to wear. This group of big, brawny men met one Sunday afternoon to pray that conditions might be better for that poor widow and her family. Right in the middle of their prayers, a big, half-grown boy came in (the son of one of the fathers who did not come) and he put down a great sack of groceries and said, "Pa couldn't come but sent his prayers." That's what we are to do again and again. Let us fortify our prayers with service. Let us undergird our appeal with cooperation. Let us answer our prayers to the last limit of our power, and then God will do the rest.

Thy will be done in earth, as it is in Heaven. Thy will be done in our homes. Let us begin there. And further back, let us begin with our own individual lives. Thy will be done with my life, and then Thy will be done in our homes, whatever that will is, without reserve. Thy will be done in our church. Thy will be done in our town, Thy will be done in our state, in our nation, in the whole world. Whatever Thy will is, oh, Father, we pray that it be brought to pass. Here are our hands, here are our feet, here are our pocketbooks, here is our loyalty, here is our love, here is our own life; all we give to Thee. Thus, should we pray.

We sometimes talk about the sacred and the secular. This is not proper talk for a Christian. There are no secularities in the right kind of a Christian life. "Whether you eat or drink, or whatsoever you do, do all to the glory of God." Go to your bank for God's glory; go to your court house for God's glory; go to your store for God's glory, or to the factory, or to the shop, or to the office, or to the farm; whatever your post of service, go there for the glory of God. Whether you eat or drink, or whatsoever you do, do all for the glory of God. That is answering this prayer. That is living the life triumphant and victorious which Christ wants everyone of his followers to live. "For me to live is Christ," said Paul. This means, For me to live is for Christ to live in me and through me. I am His and I am to do His will for the little time He wants me to stay here in the earthly arena.

Look once more at the pattern of this prayer! "Thy will be done in earth, as it is in Heaven." There is the pattern. How is God's will done in Heaven? The Bible gives us a few glimpses but they are very revealing. God's will is done joyfully in Heaven. There is not a grouch in Heaven, not one. Some have been grouches down here but when they entered within the gates of Heaven they left all the grouches behind. Thank God for that! There will never be one pessimistic grouch heard in Heaven throughout eternity. The joy of the Lord is your strength forever. "Rejoice in the Lord and again I say rejoice." "In everything with prayer and thanksgiving, let your request be made known unto God." And let joy brood over you and reign in you. Let us go joyfully, cheerfully, songfully about all our work. What if conditions are strenuous and exacting? What if adversity does come with its smiting duress? Behind the clouds there is One who lives and rules and reigns and loves. His will be done, and out of it all may He bring to pass that which will be best for us and for the glory of His name. And He will, if we relate ourselves thus joyfully and trustfully to Him.

How else is His will done above? It is done wholeheartedly. Surely there is no grudging service given yonder in

126

Heaven. Heaven is a busy place. Some think they will rest there, and they will. There will be no sense of weariness in that Blessed Home, although Heaven is to be a busy place. I love to think of the activities which will be ours when we get to Heaven! I think it would not be heavenly at all if there were nothing but idleness there. In fact, I think there will be no idlers there. His servants shall serve Him whole-heartedly. There will be no careless, half-hearted service on high. Often our service here in this life is limited, is grudg-ing, is coerced. How pitiful if we give our money to Christ's cause under duress, under hesitation! How pitiful if we give our time, our talents, our cooperation to Christ and His church, grudgingly, coercedly, hesitatingly. There will be none of that in Heaven.

If there will be no idlers in all that vast company of the redeemed through Christ's blood in the Father's House of many mansions, and we pray, "Thy will be done in earth, as it is in heaven," then we are praying that there be no idlers here among God's servants. What we are really pray-ing is, "Father, help us that none of us shall be idlers. Father, help us that none of us shall be parasites here in this world. We are passing this way but once. Help us to work, to watch and to pray. While we make this journey, Father, let us do all the good we can in all the ways we can to all the people we can down to the last hour of our journey."

And as we pray this prayer, Oh, make it personal. Let us make it personal. Are you afraid to pray it? Put that fear utterly away. Morning, noon, and night pray this great prayer, "Father, Thy will be done here on earth, as it is in Heaven. Begin, Father, with me. Thy will be done in me and through me. Whatever it means; wherever it leads; whether by life or by death; Thy will be done." And then with our homes, the same way, the same prayer. And then with our city, and with our state, and with our nation, with all the world of suffering, needy humanity; "Thy will forever be done with it all."

There are just two centers — self and Christ. Which shall it be for you? The selfish life is marked inevitably for defeat. The Christ-centered life is marked inevitably for triumph. "He always wins who sides with Christ; to Him no cause is lost." Side with Christ. Oh, hesitating soul, decide for Christ! Whatever your problem, your plight, your situation, your need, pray the great prayer and leave it unafraid in God's hand, and the right thing will come to pass as God lives.

> *Have thine own way, Lord,*
> *Have thine own way.*
> *Thou art the potter,*
> *I am the clay.*
> *Mould me and make me*
> *After Thy will,*
> *While I am waiting,*
> *Yielded and still.*

CHAPTER XI

Christ, The Cure for Trouble

C H A P T E R X I

Christ, The Cure for Trouble

~~~~~~

> *Let not your heart be troubled: ye*
> *believe in God, believe also in me.*
> —JOHN 14:1.

Many requests come to a pastor, even in a brief period of time, asking for his counsel concerning the remedy for sorrow which comes in the dark and cloudy day. And to every such troubled questioner the only helpful reply is that he or she needs to be definitely anchored to some passage, some promise, some direct quotation from the word of God, and especially be pointed to Jesus who comes with His definite assurance and with his all-sufficient wisdom, comfort and strength.

In response to this question, "What is the cure for sorrow?," many scriptures are quoted by many different persons, according to their own appraisement of various scriptures. Mr. Gladstone would have pointed the questioner to the fortieth chapter of Isaiah: "Comfort ye, comfort ye my people, saith your God." Others would point the troubled questioner to that great eighth chapter of Romans, with its confident statement: "We know that all things work together for good to them that love God." Probably more persons point the troubled questioner to the fourteenth chapter of John than to any other scripture. If the whole Bible were blotted out except that one chapter, a troubled world might still be anchored to God by that fourteenth chapter of John's Gospel.

More than the easy-going and casual observer would detect, the undertone of trial and sorrow and perplexity is heard in the world. As men are running to and fro for relief from their fears and anxieties and trials, Christ comes, as we find in this great chapter, with this sublime expression: "Let not your heart be troubled: ye believe in God, believe also in me." He is the Mediator between God and us. He is our Guide, our Helper, our Deliverer, our Redeemer, our rightful Master. Now, in view of all that is involved, He says, "Let not your heart be troubled."

You will recall how He came to utter this great word, and other comforting words to us in this whole chapter just mentioned. He said to His little band of disciples, "I am going away very soon. I must leave you." In plain words, "I am very soon to die"; and the little band was utterly dazed, stupefied, horrified. They said one to another, "He said he is going away, going to leave us, going to die. What will become of his kingdom in the world? What will become of us, who came out on his side publicly and followed him in the face of a jeering and unsympathetic world? What will be the end of his kingdom, if he is going away, going down to death?" When Jesus observed their tragic sorrow, he uttered the memorable words recorded by John in his Gospel, beginning with the expression, glorious beyond words, "Let not your heart be troubled."

Christ comes in this chapter to give a remedy, a cure for troubled lives anywhere and everywhere, whatever their plight may be, from sin or bludgeoning sorrow. He comes with His adequate remedy, Himself being the remedy. To the one who may suffer loss, and faint, and for a time fall, Christ comes with His inspiring, revealing, uplifting, all-sufficient power.

What, then, is the cure for a troubled heart? Various answers can be heard.

One answer is the answer of despair. "No cure, no help, undone, over-borne, finished" — the answer of despair. That was suggested to Job, you will recall. Wave after wave of trouble rose over the old man; his health gone utterly, his former friends gone — and instead of being sympathizers, they were cynical critics — then his own wife said, "Curse God and die." That is the answer of despair. How tragic is despair! Some are prone to accept that answer to life's trials and pain and perplexities. End it all in despair. Some are prone to take that road.

There came to the pastor of this church a letter, anonymously, saying, "My troubles overwhelm me." Many of his troubles were related in the letter. "Tell me, can I justify suicide?" If that person is in this audience today or is "listening in" anywhere, let me say to him that suicide is never justified on any ground. Suicide is self-murder. "Thou shalt not kill." Thou shalt not kill thy fellowman. That is murder. Thou shalt not kill thyself. That is self-murder. Suicide is never, never defensible, forever!

Various causes lead people to take this way out — the overwhelming failure of some business plan, the shattering of some earnestly fixed confidence. There is the downfall of some cherished program planned for by day and dreamed of by night, and all of it ends in chaos and defeat and the poor suffering victim says, "What is the use? Why go on?"

And then, worst of all, there is the driving, down-pulling power of sin in men's lives. Sin with the accusing conscience behind it. Sin with the burning memory of it all, by day and by night. Life is such a tragedy of sorrow and perplexity and sin, that often the poor short-sighted questioner says, "I will end it all by suicide." Alas! He does not end it all. He only multiplies his sorrows eternally.

Another answer quite common for the cure of trouble is Stoicism. What is the doctrine of Stoicism? That doctrine states that you are to seal your heart against all feeling. Put it away. Deaden your heart; deaden your sensibilities; deaden your emotions; refuse ever to give vent to tears; turn away from that course. Oh, how deplorable is the doctrine of Stoicism as a suggested remedy for a broken heart.

133

I wonder if you have ever read the confessions of those two great scientists who made quite a stir in the world — Darwin and Huxley? When old age came, and they began to review life, oh how pitiful were their words about their feelings; their emotions had become utterly inadequate. I read recently the confession of one of them to a Christian friend. Sunday morning came and the Christian friend said, "Come, I am going to church. Go with me." He said, "No, I never go to church, never." The friend said, "Well, go with me today." He replied, "No, but I have another thing to say. You stay with me and you talk with me the whole hour that you would be in church, about religion and what it means to you and has meant and promises to be."

The Christian friend stayed with the great scientist and told him of his simple, reliant faith in Christ through all the years and how Christ consciously became more real and precious to him every day. And this layman who had the interview with the scientist tells us that the scientist said, "I have sealed my heart all the years against all that. I would give my arm if I could feel anchored as you have just spoken to me about yourself." That was the scientist's reply to the Christian's testimony.

Another great scientist died recently. His name I need not call, for only recently have the flowers been laid upon his mound. He was an utter disbeliever, a man who talked, "No God, no angel, no spirit, no resurrection, no life beyond death and the grave which is the final chapter to human experience." And yet during the weeks of his illness, it is said authoritatively that the only thing that would quiet that man was to read to him that marvelous twenty-third Psalm: "The Lord is my shepherd; I shall not want. He maketh me to lie down in green pastures: he leadeth me beside the still waters. He restoreth my soul: he leadeth me in the paths of righteousness for his name's sake. Yea, though I walk through the valley of the shadow of death,

I will fear no evil; for thou art with me; thy rod and thy staff they comfort me," and on and on. The only thing that would quiet that nervous, distraught, dying man was to quote again and again those haunting, comforting words about our Lord. How healing as a cure for a troubled heart!

I am thinking of a lovely girl who married years ago, and after a time the husband was taken. She worked very hard and every night she would go to the movies and try to forget. Then she would go home and cry herself to sleep, without comfort.

A young man was killed in another state awhile ago, and the young bride, who had been secretly married, was overwhelmed by sorrow and she called about her a group of very worldly young people, who said, "Come, go with us to Florida, and there we will have the fragrance of the orange blossoms and every night we will have the lilt of the dance and then we will sleep in the daytime and forget it all." Oh, think of such a proposal as a cure for a broken heart!

Then, there is another proposal as a cure for a broken heart. The answer of denial. It boldly declares, "There is not any trouble; there is not any sin; there is not any suffering; there is not any pain; there is not any death. All of it is a bad thought. Forget it." That is false philosophy. I saw the helplessness of this philosophy during the first world war, when boys all around us said, "Tell us if you know, how we can die in peace." Many of them put their dying hand in the hand of the great divine Lord and went, trusting and smiling and unafraid, out on the silent sea to the land beyond. I saw there the pitiful helplessness of this denial of all the facts of life. It is much like the ostrich, putting its head in the sand, afraid to face the facts of life.

Now Jesus comes to say, "Let not your heart be troubled, ye believe in God, believe also in me. In my Father's house are many mansions. If it were not so, I would have told you. I go to prepare a place for you, and if I go and prepare a place for you, I will come again and receive you unto myself, that where I am, there ye may be also." This is the only way out of trouble, out of perplexity, out of sorrow, out of the blackest night, out of sin and sinfulness, seething about us like a great sea. It leads directly to Christ who bore the weight and the guilt of our sins in his own body upon the tree, that we, having died unto sins, might live unto righteousness.

Among the things that baffle and break the heart and perplex humanity are these three things: sin, sorrow and death. Christ comes as the remedy for all three. Christ comes as the remedy for sin: "Thou shalt call his name Jesus, for he shall save his people from their sins." A tragedy unspeakable, incomparable is the tragedy of sin, but Christ is the victor, the conqueror. He is the great Physician. He cleanses the sinful heart by his victorious, vicarious, redeeming death on the cross. Christ is the cure for sin.

Christ is the cure for sorrow. We first have to wait; be of good courage and wait: "Trust me and wait. What I do thou knowest not now; but thou shalt know hereafter." "Wait and trust me," says Jesus, "and soon the day will break and all the shadows will flee away. Cleave to me and wait."

And then there is the grim, dark hour that faces some of us practically every day, the name of which is Death. Christ comes to us and says, "Do not be afraid. Do not be dismayed. I have the keys of death and of Hades. I am watching over the welfare of every man, woman and child in the universe who will take me as Saviour and Lord. You need not be afraid, even as you die or as you see your loved ones die. You need not be frightened. I will be there to hold you, to fold you to my heart as a mother holds her frightened, sobbing child to her heart. Trust me. Fear not!"

Oh it is madness to choose any other road; it is stark madness to think you will get adequate help anywhere in the universe, apart from this divine Saviour and Lord. Is

136

He your Saviour? Are you, my friend, trusting in Him? Are you leaning on Him? Are you following Him trustfully and obediently, as best you can, wherever He leads? Be not afraid; go right on triumphantly.

But are there those of you who have no anchor; no pilot, no guide, no physician adequate, no friend able to help you? You are without God and without hope in the world! Life goes on, my friend, with its trials multiplying, its problems becoming more baffling, its burdens becoming more weighty and, yet, here comes one to you saying, "Are you willing to let me help you through all this, and to forgive your sins?" Do you want Him to give you power above yourself? Will you trust Him?

Many of your loved ones who have gone on before, from under your roof have trusted Him. Your own dear mother trusted Him unafraid. Are you willing to trust Jesus and let Him be your Saviour and let Him guide you so that your life here shall be expressed at its highest and best? Do you say, "Yes, I would like to trust Him fully; down in my heart I have trusted Him"? Then you ought to come out for Him. You ought to confess Him before men. You ought to own Him today openly, for your own sake, and for the sake of others whom your confession will help, and for the honor of the great Saviour who loved you enough to die for you. He will be your adequate helper, your adequate cure for every trouble that will ever come to you.

Who says today, "I want to follow Him. Down in my heart I have made the surrender. I want to take my place in His church"? Or do you today say, "I want to begin; I want to start; I want to make the great surrender; today I want to record my vote, my commitment, my decision for Christ"? Then He calls you!

> Be not dismayed, whate'er betide,
> God will take care of you.
> All you may need, He will provide;
> God will take care of you.

CHAPTER XII

His Own Place

His Own Place

~~~~~~

> *That he may take part of this ministry
> and apostleship, from which Judas by
> his transgression fell, that he might go
> to his own place.*
>
> —ACTS 1:25.

How many of you ever heard a sermon about Judas? You have heard about him from your cradle. Judas was the betrayer of the Divine Saviour. The worst opprobrium you can cast upon a person is to call him a Judas, a betrayer. For a long while this Judas, one of the twelve apostles, companied with Jesus and heard Him and beheld His marvelous works. Miracle after miracle performed by Jesus was evidently seen by this same Judas. And yet he betrayed Jesus for thirty pieces of silver, for about fifteen dollars of our money of today.

Covetousness swept him on and burned his soul, and the awful deed of betrayal was done. Remorse came with all its fury lashing Judas on and down so terribly that he went out and took his own life. What became of him? The text tells us. "Judas went to his own place." How plain the Bible is when it speaks on any matter!

Did you ever read Dante's description of Judas when he took his own life, and have you shuddered as you read Dante's flight of imagination as he described what Judas experienced immediately after death, and what he has experienced since, for these hundreds of years, and what he is to experience forevermore? How marvelous is the description given by Dante, page after page, with adjectives lurid and allusions terrible. But the Bible does not deal with it like that. The Bible is just as direct as words can be, and just as simple as the sunlight. Judas went to "his own place" when he died.

That is exactly where you will go and where I will go, and where every human being will go — "to his own place" — and that place will be determined this side of death. Destiny is determined this side the grave. Does not that invest our little earthly life with awful solemnity and meaning — this side the grave? Not many men and women here will live to their three score years and ten! Just a few live out that allotted time. This side those three score years and ten, or this side your three score years, or this side the half century mark, or this side, it may be, your twenty-five year mark, destiny will be determined. This side the grave, destiny will be determined. "Judas went to his own place."

Judas occupied a place here for a while that was not his own. That was not his own place when he companied with Jesus those months and months, acting the part outwardly of an apostle. He was not filling his own place. Probably the eleven other disciples thought Judas was filling his place. They probably esteemed him, cherished him in their thoughts as a brother beloved. He was a devil all the time. Jesus said so. "Have not I chosen you twelve, and one of you is a devil?"

He was a pretender. He was a deceiver. He was a man playing a game. He was a man acting a part. We cannot deceive Jesus, nor did he. Probably he deceived everybody else around him. But when death came the mask was off; the disguise was stripped aside, put away. He faced reality. He "went to his own place" when he died, and that place was determined this side of death, and when death came he was revealed. He stood out as he really was. He was in the place of his own decision, the place best fitted for him, the place he was best adapted to, the place he had chosen.

That is just what will happen with every human being when death comes. Every man will go to his own place. The judgment in the world to come, you may be sure, will marvelously reverse many human judgments. Jesus tells us so. Many that are first down here shall be last up there. Many that are last down here, shall be first up there. Many down here who have been sitting on the lower seat shall be told by Jesus: "Friend, come up higher." Dives, in all his purple and fine linen, in all his luxury and selfishness, shall be a different man in his station, in his standing, when we see him from God's viewpoint. There shall be reversals and surprises in the next world, marvelous, I do not doubt.

Many a man in this world is not in his correct place, materially and humanly speaking. Have you not heard the expression time and time again: "That man has missed his calling"? Have you not heard the expression again and again: "That person is a mis-fit"? Or "That man is a round peg in a square hole"? Often you have heard these sayings.

In all the callings about us there are misfits. There are men practicing law who ought to be preaching, and I have no doubt that there are men preaching who had better do something else. There are lawyers who ought to be teaching and there are merchants who ought to be preaching. All about us there are misfits in life, and the thing specially adapted and designed for the individual often is missed. He is out of his place. He is out of his element. The conditions and circumstances in his life have been such as to put him in a certain road which is not the right road for him.

Sometimes men who are in a wrong course, who are in an improper position or are not doing their best and highest in their place, are aroused and brought into the right place where conditions and atmosphere are all congruous and harmonious and befitting and most serviceable. But many a man here is out of his place.

If the restraints of life were all off until every man acted out just what is within him, you would know who he is and what he is. A man said in my presence one day: "I would do so and so if I were not restrained." That was the revelation of what was within him. If the restraints were all off, and you were not checked and called to account for anything by anybody, either God or man, what you would do would be what you are. If all restraints were off, that which your heart inclines you to do, the trend, the tenor, the bent of your will, your wish, your life, that is what you are.

In the world to come, we shall be revealed. At the judgment bar of God what we are shall then appear. Not only shall we give an account for the deeds done in the body, for the actions that have flowed forth from us, but for the very words of our lips, and for the very secrets of our hearts. God will bring all into judgment, and as we really are so is the judgment to reveal us. Destiny is determined this side of death.

Now, that simplifies the judgment to a remarkable degree. In other words, to an awful degree every man will be his own judge. Jesus should not be pictured as sitting yonder, tyrannical and dictatorial and cruel and arbitrary, putting this man down and that man up with some arbitrary fashion and spirit. To an awful degree every man judges his own case. To an awful degree we are to be revealed yonder. The judgment is not to determine where you are going to spend eternity. That is determined this side of the grave.

The judgment reveals you. The judgment reveals God. The judgment vindicates God to the world. There will never be a complaint against God again, when we get to the judgment and when men know the facts. When men see the basis on which God acts, when men see the meanings of the righteous judgments of God, nevermore will there be complaint against the dealings of God. He shall be vindicated then and thereafter, forevermore, in the sight of men.

People do not go to the judgment to find out where they are going to spend eternity. They will know before they get there. People are there, and revealed are they there, and likewise God in his righteous revelation is revealed there, and his ways are vindicated there, before an assembled world. There will not be a soul offering a protest to Jesus at the judgment. Not one, not one will dare to lift up a little cry and say that the judgment is unfair and unjust and arbitrary and unreasonable. Never will such a cry come from a single lip. Every one will go to his own place.

I once heard that great preacher, A. C. Dixon, tell a group of men about his going on one of the lakes in the East to preach at a camp meeting at one end of the lake, and he said: "Yonder at the other end of the lake, maybe twenty or thirty miles away, was another utterly different kind of meeting, a meeting where they raced their horses and had all forms of betting that could possibly be tolerated. A boat went out from a certain point every hour to the place of meeting; and every hour a boat went to the place of festivity and gayety and dissipation. By mistake a man came running as the boat was leaving for the camp meeting yonder, and leaped onto our boat, and the boat was soon out some distance from the shore and the people started up the old song:

> *Rock of Ages, cleft for me,*
> *Let me hide myself in Thee.*

The preacher said that the man's face paled with the pallor of death, this man who came late. And then when the song was done, somebody said: "Let us have a moment of prayer" and somebody lead in a fervent prayer, and when the prayer was finished, another said: "May I tell you of a great experience that I have had in the last week in answer to prayer, a marvelous evidence to me that God is alive and very near, and takes cognizance of the cry of His people and does actually answer prayer." And he told his story and then they had another hymn, and by that time the latecomer to the boat found the captain and said to him: "Let me off. This is intolerable to me. This is hell to me. Let me off. I am in the wrong company. I am out of my place.

If there is any place that you can let me off anywhere, get me out of this."

What would that man do in heaven? What would he do in heaven? He was unchanged. That was not his company. That was not his spirit. That was not what he liked. That was not his place. He was an utter misfit in that place of worship. The things of the Spirit were not for him. The things of the flesh, the things of the sensual, the things of the earth, those were his. All his tendencies were down-dragging. That was not his place.

That story is slightly revelatory of what it will be when we are in the "beyond." Every man will "go to his own place," that is, to heaven or to hell. The Bible is very simple about it, and the Bible is very direct about it, and the Bible is very clear about it. If a man prefers Christ, the atoning Saviour, to all other masterships, to all other allegiances, he will go where Christ is. If a man prefers self in all its forms, if he prefers mammon, if he prefers pleasure, if he prefers sin, gilded in any form, if he prefers those things to Christ and holiness and heaven, he will go to his own place. That is just as scientific as that an apple will fall downward when it leaves the tree. You have reversed every law of science or philosophy in the world if that is not so. Every man will go to his own place.

They tell us an incident about old Uncle Buck Hughes, as the people of Dallas affectionately called him. A Christian gentleman he was of the old school, a pioneer, sturdy and strong and reliable; a man the value of whose character is utterly inestimable, immeasurable; a man who had so devoted himself to the things that are highest that he shall live on and on. They tell us that a few days before he was taken ill, when a friend came to see him and they talked about the past, and then about the present, and then projected themselves in fancy on into the future, his eyes became moist and he spoke of the wife of his heart who had preceded him yonder, and with eyes moist he said: "I will be with her soon, and I will see her, and we will be together forever. And best of all I will soon see her King and mine." He has now gone "to his own place." You could not think of his being anywhere else except yonder with Christ.

We experience somewhat of heaven or hell in this present life. I know a man who has no Saviour, no hope in Christ, and I know the fear and the alarm, even terrible alarm, when illness comes to him or any of his family. All his sights are downward, and his passions are downward, and his efforts are downward. He digs for gold. He is laying up treasures earthly and material, and he has not laid up any yonder "where moth and rust cannot corrupt, and where thieves cannot break through and steal." He is of the earth. He is of time. He is of the body. He is of the visible. He is of the material. I know the trepidation and the fear that he has when he thinks of the grave. Indeed, he said to me one day: "If I were to allow myself to think of death and the grave a dozen minutes, I think I would go mad." He is carrying hell around with him now, and if he stays in that frame of mind and heart, if he stays in that atmosphere, if he stays in that character, if he stays in that world of sin, he will step out of it and gravitate to the place prepared for the devil and his angels, which is the kind of place he chose in this life. Every man must go to his own place.

I have spoken long enough. Where are you going? When you quit this house of clay, when you put off this mortal coil, where are you going? When you come some day to the last illness and are stretched upon the couch and shall leave it and go out into the shadowy beyond, where are you going? It will be determined here.

Let me tell you, dear friend, you will not get to heaven by any magic. You will not get into heaven by any legerdemain, by any sleight of hand, by any trick. There is just one way to get into heaven. It is a straight way. It is a simple way. It is a wondrous way. But you will have to take that way if you are to get there.

You cannot get into heaven by deception. "He that climbeth up some other way," said Jesus, "is a thief and a robber." You cannot get in that way. You cannot come with your pile of gold and say to the King and Saviour: "I give Thee this gold. Pass me through this gate to heaven." You cannot enter like that. You must come as a sinner, needy and helpless and dependent, undone, condemned, lost, and put your case in the hands of Him who died for just such as I have described — Himself the just, dying for the unjust; Himself the sinless, dying for the sinful; Himself the Saviour, making atonement for a helpless, condemned and lost soul. Simply, utterly, honestly, turn away from sin and self and your way of life and surrender to Him definitely, taking Him to be your Saviour His own way.

Then when you do that, that place will be your place, that Saviour will be your Saviour, heaven will be your heaven, and the people redeemed by the same blood will be your comrades. Oh, are you for Jesus? Are you for Jesus? Undone is any man who is not for Jesus. "He that is not for me is against me, and he that gathered not with me scattereth." Are you for Jesus? You will go to your own place.

I will not harrow your feelings with any attempted description of the awfulness of that state where lost people finally go. Jesus says a few things about it. Oh, just as plain as language can make it, Jesus tells us in His own simple words that those who prefer not to be for Him shall just keep on and go to their own place. They do not want Him here and they decide it. Nor will they want Him nor have Him hereafter. Character is sealed. Character settles. Habits harden. Men pass out. Death is but a slight break. Death is but a little change. Men pass through the dusty gateway called Death and out there, beyond, they are positionized as they are this side that gateway.

Oh, I ask you, which is your place? Where are you going? If right now you should gasp there where you are, and your spirit should be ushered into eternity, what would be your destination? What answer does your heart make to that inevitable question? Which will be your place, heaven or hell?

If you ask me what I have to say about it, I will say that I have not a thing to say for myself. I will say that there was never a minute that I was satisfied with myself. I will say that I cannot turn the glasses anywhere for even one minute, except with shame and with pain and with bitterness of regret that my life is not more like my Lord would have it, more unselfish, more serviceable, more Christlike. But I will go on to say that I am clinging to Christ. All other props and hopes and bridges I put aside. All other trusts I leave. I am clinging to Christ, to Christ alone. He knows I am. I am going where He is. If it is tonight, I am going where He is. If it is next year, if it is twenty-five years off, I am going where He is. Is that your place? Do you really want it to be your place? I hope you do! Where are you going? Where are you going? Have you made your eternal choice by choosing Christ? If not, will you not, even now, choose Him as your Saviour and Lord, and thus also choose heaven as your eternal home? Jesus said: "Him that cometh to me, I will in no wise cast out." Will you come to Him?

CHAPTER XIII

The Divine Necessity

CHAPTER   XIII

The Divine Necessity

~~~~~~

> *Ought not Christ to have suffered these things?*
>
> —LUKE 24:26.

JESUS was crucified on Friday morning and arose from the dead early on Sunday morning. The Gospels record eleven appearances of the risen Lord. They are as follows: to Mary Magdalene; to other women; to Simon Peter; to two disciples on the road to Emmaus; to ten apostles and others, Thomas being absent; to the eleven, Thomas being present; in Galilee; to the seven fishermen by the lakeside; to the five hundred; to James; at the ascension. Five of these appearances occurred on resurrection Sunday.

On two of these occasions Jesus cited and expounded the Old Testament scriptures (the Law, the Prophets and the Psalms) concerning Himself, especially those setting forth the divine necessity resting upon Him to make atonement for the sins of the world. These two expositions of the ancient Messianic scriptures were made to the two disciples on the Emmaus road in the late afternoon; and to the ten apostles and others later that night, assembled in a room whose doors were shut for fear of the Jews. On both occasions Jesus upbraided His hearers for their unbelief and slowness of heart to accept the testimony of the scriptures and also the testimony of those who said they had seen Him alive that very day.

The message today grows out of the profound question asked the two perplexed disciples as they journeyed along the Emmaus road, whom Christ joined after His resurrection. They were greatly perplexed and cast down. They had misunderstood the great purpose of Christ's coming. They had thought that He would reign in temporal, triumphant power. But now they thought that He was dead and in His grave in spite of the rumors they had heard that very day in Jerusalem. As Jesus walked with these perplexed men He talked with them about the prophecies concerning Him as the suffering servant, the atoning Saviour. Then He asked this vital question, "Ought not Christ to have suffered these things?"

This question calls our attention to the very heart of Christ's own divine gospel of salvation. Bound up with it are two central truths for our meditation this hour. First, the awful fact of sin; and second, God's divinely provided remedy for sin. These two facts are hard by each other all through the Holy Word of God.

First, let us consider the solemn, awful fact of sin. Men recognize the fact of sin even when they do not believe the Bible. Human laws to a remarkable degree take cognizance of sin. Individual governments form their statutes because sin must be punished. The moral conscience of the world would be shocked by the teaching that sin is not to be punished. Civilization itself will be imperilled if we withhold from sin the punishment it deserves. God has put elements within our nature which demand that sin must be punished.

Take one's memory — what haunting power there is in one's memory! It has the strange faculty of turning back the hands of the clock in one's life and reaching into the secret cabinets and unlocking them and bringing things out one would like never to think of again. God has given us memory, and its haunting power is something unspeakably pathetic. God has given us the power of conscience, and how poignant that power is at certain times in one's life! The power of conscience! Conscience may seem to sleep for a season and may seem to be dull and dead and unresponsive; but in the crucial hour, in the moral crisis, conscience makes its cry felt and heard in the most solemn and painful fashion. History, both sacred and secular, gives formal attestation to that fact.

Take the pages of Bible history — what awful chapters stand out like spectres in the night insisting upon the power of conscience! Take the case of Judas, who sold Jesus for thirty pieces of silver. After a few hours, goaded as he was to desperation by conscience, he came back to the Chief Priests, with whom the trade was made, and threw down the thirty pieces of silver with the cry, "Let us undo what we have done; I have betrayed innocent blood! Take the money back. It burns my purse; it hounds my conscience and my brain! Take it back!" They laughed him to scorn. Then, goaded by conscience, he went out and took his own life. Conscience has that awful power in human life!

George Eliot gives, in one of her books, an account of a young woman who went to shame and ruin. Earth's saddest sight is that! Here was a woman who committed murder in order to hide her shame. She put to death her illegitimate child. But a little later she was apprehended and brought to justice and judgment. Kindly women pitied her and mothered her and tried to keep her mind from dwelling on the horrible vision that had found its cumulation and culmination in her life. But whenever they paused for a moment the woman would break forth with her terrible refrain, "I hear all that you say, but will I always hear the cry of the little child that I put to death in the hedge?" It was the cry of conscience!

Conscience decrees that sin must be punished. There is an end of moral government if this be not so. What conscience cries and memory attests the Holy Word of God confirms and comes with its clear statement that all have sinned. It says, "All we like sheep have gone astray; we have turned everyone to his own way." There is no difference. "We have all sinned and come short of the glory of God."

155

"There is not a just man upon the earth that doeth good and sinneth not." And Jesus said, "Except ye repent, ye shall all likewise perish." Again he said, "Marvel not that I say unto you, ye must be born again."

All have sinned. Every human being is under the blight and poison of moral sickness. Is there any remedy? Is there any door of hope in the valley of Achor? Is there any balm in Gilead? Is there any physician who can heal this awful moral sickness which afflicts everyone? Thank God there is! The Bible states it for us in five words: "Christ died for our sins." There is the hope for beaten, sinning, suffering humanity! Christ died for our sins! Those little words state the central fact of the gospel of divine forgiveness and salvation.

Before Christ died on Calvary, every smoking altar on which lay a bird or beast in sacrifice pointed to the coming of that great sacrifice when Christ would provide a remedy for sin by the sacrifice of Himself.

Wherein does the death of Christ provide a remedy for sin? The answer to this question brings us face to face with the great doctrine of substitution, which is clearly set forth in the scriptures. Listen to some of them:

> For Christ also hath once suffered for sins, the just for the unjust, that he might bring us unto God. I Peter 3:18.

> But he was wounded for our transgressions, he was bruised for our iniquities: the chastisement of our peace was upon him; and with his stripes we are healed . . . the Lord hath laid on him the iniquities of us all. Isaiah 53:5, 6.

> Christ hath redeemed us from the curse of the law, being made a curse for us. Galatians 3:13.

> Who his own self bare our sins in his own body on the tree, that we, being dead unto sins, should live unto righteousness: by whose stripes we are healed. I Peter 2:24.

But he commendeth his love toward us, in that, while we were yet sinners, Christ died for us. Romans 5:8.

Substitution is not only a great doctrine of the Bible, but it is also one of the basic principles of life.

The other day in a hospital a lad had a tube inserted in his body and through that tube they transfused his own clear, pure, wholesome blood into the poor, emaciated body of his father. The color returned to his father's face and health and revivifying power.

Countless are the occasions on which individuals offer, yea, give their lives that others may live. How often that is true of mothers as they go down into the Valley of the Shadows in child-birth. Perhaps that is one reason for the glorification of motherhood. Surely there should be no protest upon our lips or in our hearts when we read: "For God so loved the world, that he gave his only begotten Son, that whosoever believeth in him should not perish, but have everlasting life."

Oh, why the necessity that Christ die for our sins? There are two compelling reasons for it. First, our utter helplessness to provide a remedy for sin; and second, the mighty, redemptive love of God for us, sinners though we were. So Christ died for us.

> *Jesus paid it all. All to Him I owe;*
> *Sin had left a crimson stain,*
> *He washed it white as snow.*

The deepest note in Christ's gospel is that He, the Divine Redeemer, was the vicarious and only adequate sufferer for sinners.

Why is Christ alone able to conquer our sins? First, because God, the Eternal Father, whose law we all have broken, appointed him to that divine business. Second, because Christ, the divine Son alone was spotless and sinless and able to make the perfect sacrifice. Third, because Christ

157

in his own personality is both God and man in one personality — as really God as though he were not man, and as really man as though he were not God — the God-man in one personality. For these reasons he is able to be the one adequate Mediator to win sinners back to God.

Oh, think of Him, dying for you. Think how they took Him and laid aside His robe and scourged Him and carried Him up the hill — the Christ — and nailed Him to the cross — and there 'twixt Heaven and earth He died — the Friend of sinners died! It was for you! There is not any way out for you and me, except through that sacrifice of Christ. No wonder the great old John Newton sang:

> In evil long I took delight,
> Unawed by shame or fear,
> Till a new object struck my sight
> That stopped my wild career!
>
> I saw One hanging on a tree
> In agony and blood!
> He fixed His languid eye on me
> As near that cross I stood!
>
> Oh, never to my latest breath
> Can I forget that look —
> It seemed to charge me with His death
> Though not a word He spoke.
>
> My conscience felt and owned my guilt —
> And drove me to despair.
> I knew my sins His blood had spilt
> And helped to nail Him there.
>
> A second look He gave, which said:
> I freely all forgive!
> This blood is for thy ransom paid.
> I died that thou mightest live!

That thou mightest live! What if you refuse Him? God forbid! God forbid, my dear, dear friends, that even one in this audience should refuse to believe in Christ, the atoning Redeemer from sin! A compelling and divine necessity was upon Him to suffer and die for you and thereby make available for you full pardon for your sins and eternal salvation for your soul. Will you accept what He has done for you and what He freely offers you? May your answer be the joyful "Yes" of your heart! Say it now so that men on earth, and the angels in heaven, and the Lord Himself will know that you mean it.

CHAPTER XIV

Peace Be Unto You

CHAPTER XIV

Peace Be Unto You

~~~~~~

And as they thus spake, Jesus himself stood in the midst of them, and saith unto them, Peace be unto you.
—LUKE 24:36.

THIS is one of the most notable appearances of our Lord, after His resurrection. He made eleven distinct and different appearances during the forty days of His sojourn on the earth after He was risen from the dead. This is one of the most suggestive and instructive of all his appearances.

He appeared, you remember, first of all to Mary; then He appeared to other women; He made an appearance to Simon Peter. Later He appeared to the two disciples on the way to Emmaus, and they hurried back to the followers of Jesus who were in an upper room conversing and reasoning about all these matters. While they talked Jesus stood in their midst and confirmed the several reports which had reached them touching the fact that He had verily risen from the dead. But still all of them did not believe it. Some of them did, for unto some of them He had appeared and already they were convinced. But others of them were terrified and affrighted and imagined that a ghost had made its appearance among them. They were still terrified as He began to speak to them.

Several vital truths emerge from this incident. First, is the certainty of the resurrection of Jesus Christ from the grave. Of all the facts of history, I hazard nothing in saying that there is no more thoroughly authenticated fact in all history than the resurrection of Jesus Christ from the grave. My conviction is that He verily came out of the grave, put death beneath His feet, and after forty days ascended to Heaven where He ever lives to make intercession for us.

A man has to discredit all testimony and has to discard all the laws of evidence if he repudiates or calls in question the great teaching of the resurrection of Jesus from the grave. There is one question at which unbelief stumbles and staggers; that question is: What became of the body of Jesus? Where is the body of Jesus? I repeat, a fact as thoroughly authenticated as any fact in all history is the fact that Jesus of Nazareth, crucified under Pontius Pilate, and buried in Joseph's new tomb, on the third day came out of the grave, a triumphant man, a triumphant God, over the power of death. And every one who has set out with honest mind and heart to find out the truth of that matter has been convinced beyond the shadow of a doubt of the truth of that claim.

Gilbert West, that noted skeptic, said, "I will overthrow the whole scheme of the Christian religion by overthrowing the teaching that Jesus of Nazareth came out of the grave, raised from the dead." He began this project with the result that, after faithful investigation, he bowed before Jesus Christ and sought forgiveness of his sins. Then the noted unbeliever became one of the most triumphant soldiers and witnesses for Jesus Christ in all the earth.

So must we always accept the proposition that if Christ be not risen from the dead, Christianity is a farce and a delusion from first to last. Paul was right when he said, "If He be not risen, our preaching is vain; we are yet in our sins, and we are of all men most miserable." The more you look into this proposition and ponder its testimony, the more your mind and your heart will be overwhelmed with the conviction and the consciousness that our Lord is not in the grave. He has put the grave beneath His feet, and is ascended on high, and now reigns and lives and intercedes for all whom the Father hath given Him.

But there are some lessons in this simple narrative of this fifth appearance of Jesus after His resurrection. He came to this company of dismayed disciples, and gave them several evidences of His resurrection. He gave them the evidence of hearing. He gave them the evidence of seeing. He gave them the evidence of touching. He gave them the evidence of common sense. And all these evidences stand out in this portion of scripture.

Jesus appeared to these disciples, stood in their midst unannounced and at the very first sight of Him, they heard him say, "Peace be unto you." He gave them, first of all, the evidence of hearing. There must have been something about the voice of Jesus that never echoed in any other voice. There must have been something about His speech that no man could imitate. Thus when he stood in their midst and said, "Peace be unto you," they were terrified; they were affrighted; they thought a ghost had made its appearance.

Then he continued, in effect: "Why are ye troubled, and why do ye have reasonings in your heart? I am but carrying out what Moses and the prophets foretold — all this is but the unfolding, the revealing, the opening of the things that were foretold should thus come to pass." And still they wondered, and still they were amazed, and still they were filled with fear. O, how slow to believe were even the apostles! Slow to believe! No wonder He cried out, "O, foolish men, and slow of heart to believe!"

And then He gave them the evidence of sight. "Why are ye terrified? I am not a ghost. I am not an apparition. I am not a mere spirit. Look on me; behold that it is I, myself." And He showed them the nail-prints in His hands and feet and the rent in His side.

One week later Jesus appeared again in their meeting and said to Thomas, who was not in the first meeting, "Thomas, thou doubting, distrusting, unbelieving one, come hither and put your fingers in the nail prints in my hands and feet, and thrust your hand into the great rent in my side from which issued blood and water as I died on the tree. Come, handle me. Not only hear me, and not only look upon me, but come and touch me." A spirit does not have bones and flesh. A spirit does not have corporal existence. "Come and touch me, and see for yourself that I am Jesus risen from the dead."

Then, as if to give them the crowning proof of the certainty of the resurrection, Jesus appealed to their common sense. "Have ye anything here to eat?" He asked. "Bring it to me." And they brought Him a piece of fish and an honeycomb, and there before them, the Master did eat. And yet they were terrified and affrighted through it all, until, at the last, they were overwhelmed and convinced that He was verily risen from the grave.

The one great fact in which we rejoice is the fact of the resurrection of Jesus Christ from the grave. That is the great key-stone in the arch, for the redemption of a ruined world. We rejoice in it. Without cavil or fear, without distrust, we build our hope upon this fact that Christ who was in the grave, has been raised from the dead and has become the first fruits of them that slept.

When once this great fact of the resurrection of Jesus Christ is conceded, Christianity is accepted and all other facts of any moment in the Christian religion are adjusted. Why need men have doubts about miracles, if Christ came out of the grave? Why need men wonder about supernaturalism, if this one great fact be granted? But if this fact be denied, if this fact be repudiated, the whole great superstructure of the Christian religion shall totter and fall into ashes and death; for, if Jesus be in the grave, our gospel is a delusion, and we are of all men most miserable.

Let us look at Jesus' character after His resurrection. These verses here indicate the character of Jesus after He had been dead, and after He had come out of the grave, and had put death beneath His feet. What will He think of us now? How will He act now? What relation will He bear to us now? We see that after His resurrection, just as He was before His death, Jesus was still desirous that His followers might have peace. The very first word He spoke when He stood in that upper room where the apostles and friends were gathered was "Peace be unto you." And time and time again, when He met the apostles after His resurrection, His greeting always was, "Peace be unto you." And so in this incident, as we see Him appearing to this company of apostles, His usual salutation falls upon their ears and upon ours, "Peace be unto you." Our Lord Jesus, after His resurrection, was concerned, just as He was before, that we might have peace.

Jesus does not want us to be filled with foreboding and depression and despondency and distrust and gloom. His words were and are, "Rejoice. Be of good cheer. Be not cast down. Be not consumed with anxious care. Put distrust and doubt and unbelief far away." That was the mind and heart of our Lord, after He rose from the grave, just as it was before and just as it is even now.

We see also in this manifestation that He sought to drive away all doubt and distrust. "Why are ye troubled?" He tenderly inquired. "Why are ye cast down?" And in that tender, searching inquiry, our Master sought to drive away all unbelief and all distrust. "O, ye of little faith! Why do you doubt?" Doubt consumes; doubt depresses; doubt enslaves; doubt harms; doubt hurts. Put your doubt and your distrust and your unbelief far away. There is no occasion for it.

Thus we see in these scriptures that Jesus had the same loving fellowship with men after the resurrection that He had before His death. Think what fellowship our Lord had with men! He mingled with all classes of people. Here He dined; there He comforted; here He healed; there He warned; here he preached; and there He taught. These things He did among all kinds of people — high and low, rich and poor, young and old, good and bad. Children loved Him because they instinctively knew that He loved them.

So after He was risen from the dead He mingled with men just as before. "Have ye anything to eat?" He asked. And our Lord sat down with that company of devoted friends and ate as He did before His death. O, the fellowship of Jesus! O, brethren, born for adversity, He has a heart of sympathy for you. He had commiseration and companionship and fellowship for them after death, as well as before!

Notice here the patience of our Master with His people. How slow they were to believe! How slow they were to accept Him! How hesitant they were to acknowledge Him as Lord and Master. But He was patient with them. He revealed little by little, until men more and more came to an understanding of who He was.

See again, friends, how our Lord after His resurrection was concerned about scripture. He sat down there on this occasion and told them, "Did I not tell you before my death that all these things must be fulfilled, which were spoken by Moses and by the prophets and in the Psalms? And now I point you back to the great living word of God! That was what I told you then, and after my resurrection, I tell it to you again." Oh, the tender regard our Lord had for the divine Word; and in that there ought to be a lesson for us.

Why should we accept, unreservedly, many of the great facts of the Old Testament which unfriendly critics of the Bible so ardently dispute? Why do we accept, unreservedly, the great fact of man's fall? Because Jesus Christ magnified that awful fact in His teachings, while among men. Why do we accept the fact of the great flood that covered the earth in Noah's time? Because our Lord accepted it and drew some of His greatest lessons from it. Why do we accept the fact of the great disasters that came to Sodom and Gomorrah in the days of Lot? Because our Lord accepted it, and based some pointed lessons on it. Why do we accept the teaching that the great fish swallowed Jonah, where Jonah abode for three days? Why do we accept it? We accept it, unreservedly, because Christ accepted it, and drew some of the most pungent lessons of His public ministry from it.

And whatever our Lord hath endorsed, unreservedly we endorse. He endorsed the great facts of scriptural history. We follow Christ Jesus in His acceptance of all these great facts, and do not follow the so-called critics; for our Lord knew the sure and infallible oracles of God. Having risen from the dead, Jesus had the same tender regard for scripture that He had before. He quoted and explained both the Law and the Prophets after His resurrection just as He had done before His crucifixion.

Risen from the dead, He was concerned, just as He was before, for the salvation of men. O, friends, our Lord, when He died on the cross, ah, surely, He was concerned for the lifting up of a ruined, doomed, lost race! And He is just as much concerned now. Risen from the dead, He stands with His company of disciples, and teaches them the great plan of salvation just as He taught before. This was the divine commission that He, on this occasion, gave these disciples: "As my Father hath sent me, even so send I you." Find out why Jesus came, and you find out for what you came to the Kingdom. The redeemed of the Lord are one in their mission with Jesus of Nazareth. The only reason we need not die for a lost world, as our Lord did, is that in Him was full atonement made for a ruined race; and by living, by working, and by doing, we can do more than by dying. Otherwise, we ought to die for the redemption of men — for a ruined world. Our Lord was and is the same great, mighty missionary Leader, the same great world-wide gospel propagandist after His resurrection, that He was before.

And now, a final word: What do these scriptures teach of our own resurrection? It remained for Christianity to give us the great truth that our bodies should be raised from the grave. Before Jesus came there were glimmerings of light, that the spirit should live forever. But it remained for Christianity to give us that great hope, that marvelous, unapproachable truth that these bodies should be raised from the grave. Christianity means to redeem the entire man. Christ came to seek and to save the lost. Our bodies are lost as well as our spirits. Christianity came to redeem these bodies. After a while they shall be fully regenerated as are our spirits, and shall come back together, forever to be with the Lord.

Our future nature, after death, is to be one filled with peace. We shall have fellowship with each other and recognition beyond the grave. Often the question is asked, "Will God's children know each other in heaven?" It would be difficult to ask a more foolish and unreasonable question. We shall certainly not know less in heaven than we know here on earth. To be sure, we will know each other, and social life shall be extended and rejoiced in in heaven infinitely beyond its highest conception on earth. Yes, just as Jesus came and knew and as these men in the flesh knew the resurrected Lord, so shall all redeemed by His blood know, and greet and rejoice with each other on the golden shore. The child shall climb up in your arms, and you will call it your child again. And the loved one, separated from you, shall sit down by you, and you will talk over the glad days again.

The resurrection of Jesus carries with it the great doctrine of our resurrection, and of our recognition and our fellowship on the other shore. That is one of the sweetest truths in our Christian religion. "We shall know, even as we are known," and we shall do just like our Lord did. We shall talk of the past, for we shall remember. He remembered the past and dwelt upon it. So shall it be in our Father's house on high.

And there is this other word: We shall be busy in our resurrection life. I do not know where we shall go. I do not know on what missions He will send us. You and I may be preachers to some far-off planet after we go to be with God. But we shall be busy. Heaven is a place of unwearied activity. Our Lord will be there, and we shall work with Him and for Him forever.

Is the resurrection and the life your portion? It is, if you are Christ's. Are you Christ's? This is the all-important matter. Are you Christ's? Do you belong to Him? Have you accepted Him as your personal Saviour? Come now and hear Him say, "Peace be unto you."

171